Assessment in the Learner-Centered Classroom

Alan Trussell-Cullen

Dominie Press, Inc.

Publisher: Raymond Yuen
Editor: Bob Rowland
Designer: Gary Hamada
Illustrator: Richard Pinson

Copyright © 1998 Dominie Press, Inc. All rights reserved. Reprinted 2004.

No part of this publication may be reproduced or transmitted in any form or by any means without permission in writing from the publisher. Reproduction of any part of this book, through photocopy, recording, or any electronic or mechanical retrieval system, without the written permission of the publisher, is an infringement of the copyright law.

Published by:

Dominie Press, Inc.
1949 Kellogg Avenue
Carlsbad, California 92008 USA

ISBN 0-7685-0017-6
Printed in The United States of America
2 3 4 5 6 W 06 05 04

Table of Contents

Introduction

The Learner-Centered Classroom

The history of education is littered with worn-out phrases and yesterday's buzzwords. In previous eras, we pursued the experience-based classroom, the open-plan classroom, the integrated classroom, the creative arts classroom, the liberal arts classroom, and more recently, the whole-language classroom. Not that we should be cynical or disparaging about these changes of focus; each in its own way has made a contribution to our collective body of knowledge about how learners learn.

And now we talk about the learner-centered classroom.

Perhaps it is important to remember that we haven't always been convinced that schools exist primarily for learning. Down through history, the dominant purpose of education has varied with the culture and the historical imperatives of the times. At one time or another, schools have been seen as institutions for furthering morality, consolidating the power of the church, teaching manners, civilizing the savage mind, and inculcating the virtues of patriotism, nationalism, communism, or a host of other "isms." Schools have been baby-sitting institutions, taking care of children so their parents could work in factories. They have been seen as a means of preparing people for a craft, a trade, a job, a profession, or for marriage, for leadership, for life. They've been accused of perpetuating snobbery and social class distinctions as well as educating the masses and indulging in social engineering.

So why learner-centered classrooms?

Because right now, at this point in our history, our community sees as the main function of our schools the fostering and facilitating of learning.

Consequently, the children who attend our schools are seen as learners. They are the center of this educational universe; not the teachers and administrators, and certainly not the vast army of researchers and specialists and consultants who service our schools. Good schools are where children learn, where classrooms are learner-centered, and where the instruction is designed around, and geared to meeting, the learning needs of the students.

But if learning is our core business, then to satisfy ourselves that we are doing a good job and to satisfy the community that is paying us to do this job, we have to be able to know and show that our students are learning. Because of this, learner-centered classrooms have to have effective systems of assessment.

Our schools are undergoing constant change–change that affects curriculum, methodology, teacher education, resources, and philosophy. Yet the one area that seems to have been most resistant to change has been that of assessment. Change in this area has been slow, not because of the lack of fresh teacher ideas about assessment practice, but because teacher and community beliefs about assessment have been slow to change.

Teachers generally tend to be practical people. They have to be to survive! They don't always welcome quantities of theory–they like to get on with the job. That's why they prefer to go to workshops rather than lectures. They like things that are described as "hands on." They think teaching is what you *do.*

Well, so it is. But what we *think* and *believe* begets what we do. And if we are going to change what we do, or even just run a close check on what we do, we may have to first take a good hard look at some of our ideas and our beliefs about what we do.

Sadly, many of the traditional things we've ended up doing in the name of assessment have been: (a) time-consuming; (b) of dubious validity; (c) frequently meaningless to the learner; and worst of all, (d) haven't in any significant way helped the learner to *learn*!

One major misconception that persists about assessment is that it is something that has to be separate from learning. The thinking goes like this: we teach the students something, they learn it, and then we test them to see what they've learned. That's the assessment part! Right?

Wrong!

In fact, good teachers assess learning all the time. We ask questions. We observe responses. We check understandings. We structure activities that will not only extend learning but also expose it for diagnosis. We reflect on the learning. We help the students to reflect, too. We keep examples of the learning products in order to document the learning progress.

One of the key messages we hope to convey in this book is that it is more effective and efficient to do assessment–not as a separate process but in an organic way–as part of the instruction and the learning.

Another major misconception we have let persist is that there is only one way to assess learning, and that is with a test. Our community in the main still believes that. Many of our teachers still do, too.

This doesn't mean that traditional standardized tests haven't had their critics over the years. But even when we took those criticisms on board, we still tended to think about assessment with our minds in "test mode." We tried to replace the old tests with "better" new tests. When those didn't work, we sought to find test "substitutes." For example, observational assessment and portfolio assessment have suffered from being conceived of as "alternatives" to, or substitutes for, testing. In other words, we were still thinking we needed one single instrument or approach to achieve our learning assessment needs.

In this book, we set out to show teachers how to use a multi-strategied approach to assessment. Instead of one single assessment instrument, we encourage teachers to use a wide range of assessment tools to gather the data we need to know and show that our students are learning. We gather all these together in a multi-strategied Learning Assessment Toolbox.

To help teachers do this, the book takes the reader step by step through a systematic learning and assessment planning process.

Book Overview

Chapter 1	In Chapter 1, we examine prevailing conceptions and misconceptions about assessment and the implications for running an effective learning-centered classroom.
Chapter 2	We need to know who we are doing this assessment for, and why. In Chapter 2, we set about preparing an assessment audit for our learners.
Chapter 3	We want to show that assessment needs to be seen as an integral, or organic, part of learning and instruction. In Chapter 3, we begin to plan learning in a systematic way.
Chapter 4	In Chapter 4, we plan the specific assessment strategies and tools we are going to use in assessing our learning goals.
Chapter 5	Now we are ready to begin putting it all to work in our classrooms. In Chapter 5, we draw up a schedule to make sure it all happens when we need it. We also consider ways to involve students and parents in a collaborative and empowering partnership.
Chapter 6	Teachers need assessment strategies to give them detailed feedback so they can continuously monitor and fine-tune the learning and the instruction. But administrators need to be able to survey the learning in the school for accountability purposes, too. In Chapter 6, we show how the classroom assessment record can be used to derive the group "snapshot" surveys that administrators need.
Chapter 7	It won't always happen smoothly. There are bound to be glitches and challenges of one kind or another. In Chapter 7, we look at some of the main questions and difficulties that may arise and offer suggestions for dealing with them.
Chapter 8	In Chapter 8, we take stock of ourselves. What have we learned? How far have we come? Where do we go from here? Then we give ourselves a "giant pat on the back" for a job well done.

Who is this book for?

Assessment in the Learner-Centered Classroom can be used in a number of different ways:

- Individual teachers, all on their own, can follow this assessment process with their students in the classroom.
- A group of teachers within a school can meet together to develop their own collaborative version of this process.
- A school faculty can work together collaboratively to develop this assessment process for the whole school.
- A whole district may also choose to bring representatives together from different schools to plan and develop their own district-wide learning assessment process.
- In fact, a whole state or country could embark on this kind of exercise, too! Hallelujah!

But let's start at the beginning.

One of my colleagues recently declared that "assessment is the most boring subject in the world!" On its own, the subject may seem dry, but when assessment and learning are thought of together, exciting things begin to happen. Teachers gain ownership of the whole learning and assessment process. They share that ownership with their students and their students' parents. Teachers become excited–more than excited: they become *passionate!* They share and collaborate with their colleagues. Together, they begin to create something truly wonderful–a learning community!

Let's begin...

Getting Ready

What Is Assessment and Why Do We Do It?

In This Chapter

- Act One, Scene One, Take One...
- Assessment Anxiety
- Defining Our Terms
- The Learning Assessment Process
- Other Assessment Terms
- There's a Jungle of Misconceptions about Assessement Out There!
- How Did All These Misconceptions Come About?
- Once Upon An Assessment Time: A Brief History of Assessment Beliefs and Practices
- From Kidwatching to Portfolios
- Are Portfolios Enough?
- Assessment Mind-Sets We Need to Change
- So, What Do We Really Want from Our Assessment System?
- We Do It In Four Easy Steps
- "But wait! I'm only a classroom teacher! Can I do this all by myself?"
- This Is an Adaptable and Inclusive Approach to Learning Assessment
- Chapter Review: Multiple-Choice Nightmares

Act One, Scene One, Take One...

The scene: My classroom on a typical school morning. The cast members are assembled, all sitting at their desks.

Action: I start the day by giving out some papers and telling the children as I go that they're going to have a test on the book they've been reading. They seem to accept this. Most of them sort of shrug their shoulders and get out their pens, ready to write–some even appear eager.

One or two of my students look a little apprehensive. And so they should. Judging by past experiences, I'm sure they haven't completed the required reading. That would have meant getting organized, and these particular kids just don't do that very well.

Then there's Mike and Glenda over in the corner. Now, they're going to find this test hard, not because they haven't tried to do the reading assignment, but because they're poor readers. Mike isn't even going to be able to sit still long enough to complete the test. He suffers from ADD (Attention Deficit Disorder). Everyone knows that. Even Mike. Whenever any of the other teachers talk about Mike, they refer to him as "that ADD kid in your room." It's as if he has this label stitched into his sweater or tattooed on his forehead.

And Glenda? Well, she has no confidence, no self-esteem. She'll look at the paper and maybe check the odd box; then she'll cross that out. Then she'll check the same box again. Pretty soon, she'll give up and just sit there and wait until the test time is all used up. Here's hoping she doesn't burst into tears. She used to do that all the time at the start of the year, but I managed to stamp that out. Now she just sits there. (I have this awful feeling she's still crying, only on the inside.)

The one child I really fear is Abigail. Every class has its Abigail–if you're both lucky and unlucky! Out of the corner of my eye I see her hand go up–right on cue!

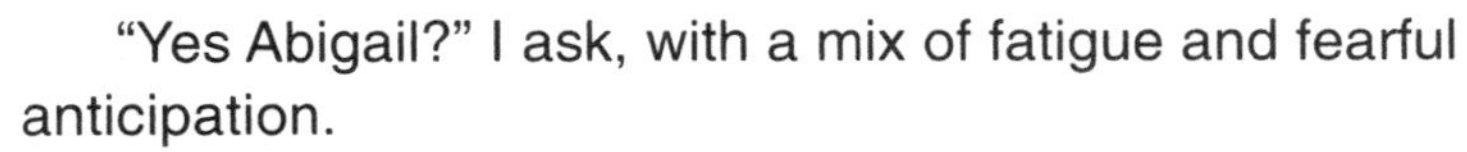

"Yes Abigail?" I ask, with a mix of fatigue and fearful anticipation.

"Why do we have to have a test on the book?"

I might be thrown a little by this direct approach, but I'm sure as heck not going to show it! After all, I'm the teacher! I'm the one in charge! I'm the one who asks all the questions! Abigail's look says I'm supposed to be the one who knows all the answers, too!

"To see if you've read it, Abigail," I say, smiling encouragingly.

"But you know we've read it," says Abigail. "We all read it in class."

"Yes, but I don't know if you understood it all," I say patiently.

"But we've talked about it," says Abigail. "We couldn't have talked about it if we didn't understand it. And anyway, if we don't understand it, how's a test going to help us understand it all the more?"

"The test isn't supposed to help you!" My voice is becoming a little fraught. I'm also somewhat surprised by what I just heard myself say! Abigail has heard it, too. Like the hotshot attorney she's probably going to be one day, she rises to address the judge and jury.

"Then who is it supposed to help?" she asks the class in general.

This is going to be tough. I suck in some air and go on the attack.

"It's supposed to help me so I can help you!"

I smile inside–that came out all right. I rest my case, your honor. But Abigail isn't finished with me yet.

"We won't always have you to help us," she says.

"Abigail," I say with a firmer tone and marshaling a little more fire power along my threatened border. "You're holding the class up now."

"I just want to know why we have to do this. I really wanted to get on and read the next chapter." Abigail puts her head down and picks up her pen. She knows she's beaten–for now. Just as I know I've won. But why does it feel like I only won by cheating? And what was that about wanting to read on. Isn't that what I'm really trying to achieve here–to get them so enthused and excited by literature that they'll want to read, they'll need to read, they'll be dying to read?! And here's Abigail, saying she'll read on, not because of me, but in spite of me because I feel I have to give them a test, because I'm a teacher and that's what teachers do!

But why am I giving them a test, really? I already know they've read the book. And I know which children really grasped what the writer was trying to say from the way they talked about it and from the fun dramatization we did the other day.

As for Mike–well, maybe thinking about his ADD wasn't fair in this case, because he seemed to get very involved in the story. He even took a part in the dramatization–and he was good!

And Glenda? Well, I know she liked the story. She got that daydreamer look and then asked if she could draw a picture about it. In fact, that's one way Glenda does seem to be able to respond to things. Maybe I should help her get to ideas and words via drawing.

Maybe you're right, Abigail! What's the test going to tell me that I don't already know?

Maybe that's where I should start–from what I already know about the children.

You know, sometimes when I look around my classroom, I think the dumbest person here is me!

Close up of teacher's thoughtful expression.
Slow fade to commercial break...

Assessment Anxiety

Teachers are busy people. That's because, depending on how many kids we have in our class, there's a potential for twenty to thirty different revolutions about to break out at any given minute of the teaching day!

We also have obligations to our school administrators and our colleagues across the hall.

And, of course, there are the parents of the kids we teach, who are always wanting to know how their children are progressing–or worse, why they're not progressing faster. Or even worse still, why the heck are we holding their little genius back!

Parents are a subset of a larger set known as "the community" who like to scrutinize what we're doing, even if it's just to make sure their taxes are being spent wisely. They're also inclined to hold us personally and entirely responsible for the next generation. If we don't get it right in our classrooms, the end of the world is going to be nigh, and, "Teacher, it's going to be all your fault!"

Oh, and by the way–besides being teachers, we're also supposed to be free and fun-loving human beings who have obligations to our families and friends, and possibly our own kids, who just happen to want it all–only they want it all now!

So who needs to sleep at night?

The nub of our problem is that our job in the classroom is not teaching. We've been wrongly labelled.

You see, it's not what *we* do that matters–it's what the *kids* do.

They're there to learn, and we're there–to use an old-fashioned term–to *learn* them!

In other words, "learning" is our bag, not teaching. And if we don't like the word *bag*, how about our *speciality*, or our *raison d'etre*, or our *gift to the community*, our *art form*, our *metier*, our *area of craft*. However we put it, what we do is help people learn.

The problem is, given the terribly insecure and disturbed world we live in, how do we prove that learning is really happening?

The principal wants to be sure we're doing our job. The parents want to know. The community wants to know. And, of course, *we* want to know. As a teacher, I want to know because, if what I am doing is working, I want to keep on doing it. And if what I am doing is not working, I want to stop and do something else.

Of course, we have some grand names for what we're talking about here. Those with a good ear for jargon will talk about ASSESSMENT and EVALUATION. But we have more colloquial terms for it, too–like *grading, report cards, marking,* and *testing.*

The fact of the matter is, assessment has grown into the number-one nightmare for teachers. There ought to be an acronym for it. How about AA (Assessment Anxiety), or ADD (Assessment Delirium Disorder)?

Defining Our Terms

Writers in this field sometimes make a distinction between assessment and evaluation.

- Assessment is seen as the gathering of evidence and documentation of the learning.
- Evaluation is viewed as the process whereby we seek to interpret the assessment data and make appropriate professional judgments based on that data.

While such a distinction has some theoretical validity, in practice it is not very helpful. In the classroom, the two are interwoven, not only with each other but also with the learning itself. In fact, one of our major concerns in this book is to encourage teachers to see assessment and evaluation, not as something separate from learning, but as an integral and "organic" part of one continuous process.

There are three critical areas, or aspects, to learning:

- Learning involves knowledge and understanding. So assessment involves answering the question: "What do the learners already know and understand, and what do they *need* to know and understand?"
- Learning involves skills and strategies. So assessment involves answering the question: "What can the learners already do, and what do they *need* to be able to do?"
- Learning involves attitudes and values. So assessment involves answering the question: "What do the learners think and feel and believe about what they are learning, and about themselves as learners?"

The teacher and student collect evidence and documentation for each of these aspects of learning, and as part of the same process, they evaluate the data. This involves three aspects, too:

- The valuing of the data. The teacher and student ask: *How typical, valid, or reliable is this data?*
- The interpretation of the data. The teacher and student ask: *What does it all mean?*
- The seeking of implications for instruction. The teacher and student ask: *What do I do about it?*

While there will be transitions and changes of emphasis as the learning unfolds, we prefer to refer to this whole process as the Learning Assessment Process. Consequently, throughout this book, when we refer to assessment, we have in mind this broader definition that also encompasses evaluation. The diagram below seeks to summarize the Learning Assessment Process as we conceive of it for the purposes of this book.

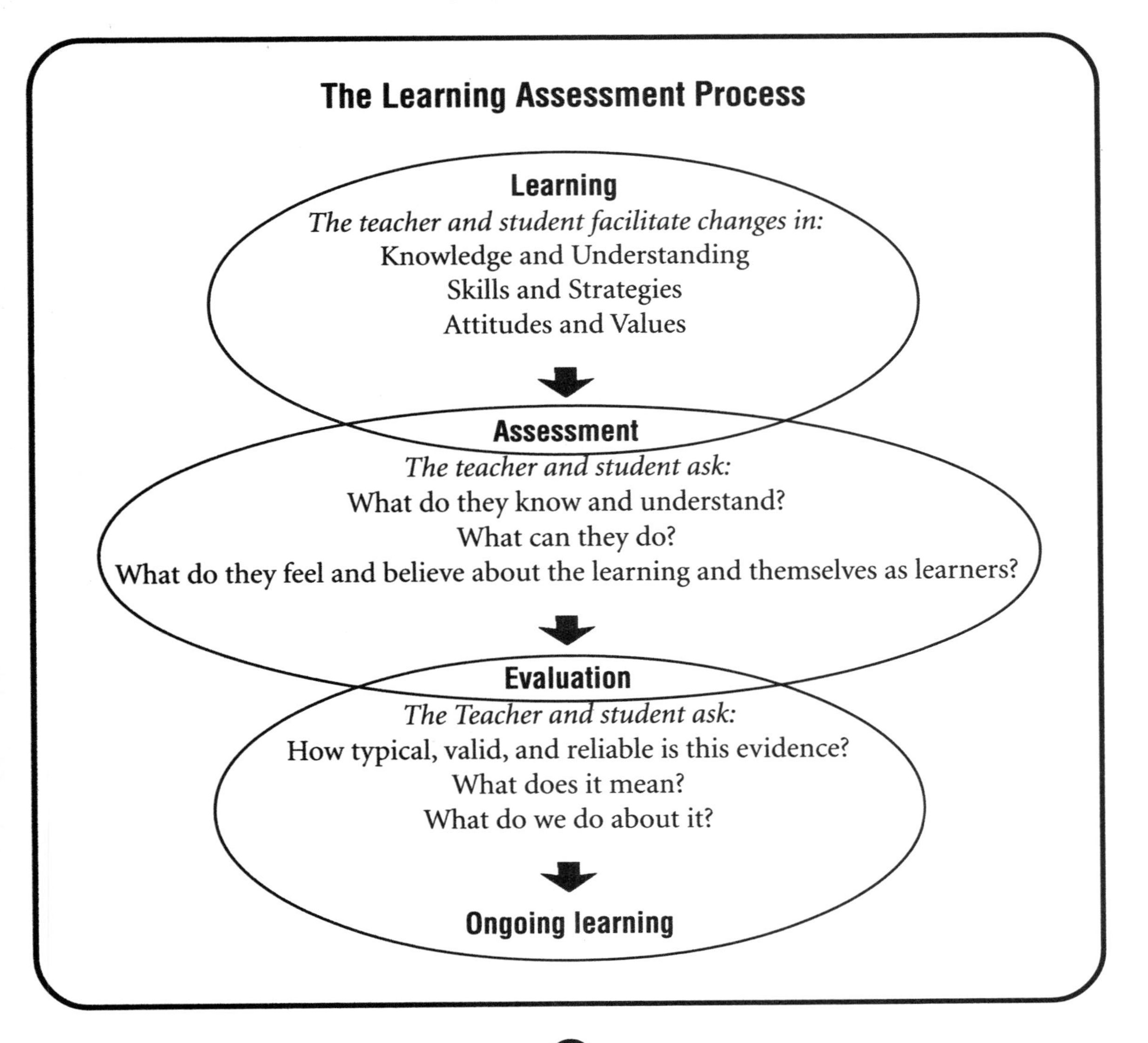

The Learning Assessment Process
Learning
The teacher and student facilitate changes in:
Knowledge and Understanding
Skills and Strategies
Attitudes and Values
Assessment
The teacher and student ask:
What do they know and understand?
What can they do?
What do they feel and believe about the learning and themselves as learners?
Evaluation
The Teacher and student ask:
How typical, valid, and reliable is this evidence?
What does it mean?
What do we do about it?
Ongoing learning

Other Assessment Terms

Of course, there are other terms we use to apply to this field. We talk about monitoring, surveying, grading, marking, and testing.

Monitoring

By monitoring, we mean "keeping an eye on the learning" or following it as it progresses. The implication in monitoring is that we are somewhat detached or objective about the learning process. The assessment approach we will be describing in this book is far from detached. We will be talking about assessment as an interactive and organic part of learning. When we do use the term *monitoring* in this book, we are referring to this narrower and specific idea of following and keeping an eye on the learning, rather than the more global concept of assessment.

Surveying

A survey is a group snapshot of the learning–what the group knows and is able and attitudinally empowered to do at one point in time. We will talk about this in more detail in Chapter 6.

Grading

The word *grading* is often used as a synonym for *assessment.* As the reader will quickly discover, we do not like this term. The reasons for this will become obvious later in this chapter!

Marking

Marking is often used as a synonym for *assessment,* too. The word has metaphorical origins. The teacher leaves a mark to show the work has been seen. Unfortunately, the word has other metaphorical connotations that aren't so flattering. For example, many species of animal indulge in marking. They leave their mark to indicate their territory! Graffiti artists leave their tag, or their mark, too. The term even carries connotations of disfigurement. In case it is not already obvious, we don't like this term much, either.

Testing

Testing is another word that is frequently used as a synonym for *assessment.* This is because traditionally, the "test," especially the "standardized test," has been the one, and often the only, assessment instrument. While conceding that tests do have a place in assessment strategies, the test is only one small part of the assessment universe. There are many other strategies and assessment tools that we can use. So when we talk about testing in this book, we are referring only to the setting and taking of tests.

There's a Jungle of Misconceptions about Assessment Out There!

The difficulty we might encounter while we're trying to clarify our thoughts about all these things is that we are all susceptible to powerful metaphors and the prevailing ideas and beliefs of our times. Often we accept the conventional wisdom of our community without examining it too closely; and often this isn't a problem because conventional wisdom can sometimes be very sensible and wise!

Unfortunately, when it comes to the conventional wisdom about assessment, it has been singularly unhelpful. Traditional approaches to assessment have left us with a number of major misconceptions. We need to clear these up and send them packing before we settle down to saying what we should be thinking and doing about assessment.

Misconception number 1

We tend to think of assessment as something that we do *after* the learning is finished, or something that *interrupts* the learning, or is in some way separate from the learning.

The familiar formula goes like this:

We teach the kids something,
they learn it, and then
we test to see what they've learned.

(That's the assessment part!)

Reality check!

In good teaching, assessment is something that is going on all the time as part of the teacher's natural ongoing interaction with the learners' responses. That's why we question, we listen, we observe what they do, we encourage this and discourage that, praise this, ignore that–all of these things we're doing as good teachers are really assessment strategies!

We do it naturally and it is an organic part (There's that word again!) of the whole learning process. In fact, what we need to do is think about this as part of a planning/ teaching/ learning/assessing/ evaluating/ planning/ teaching etc. spiral.

Misconception number 2

We tend to think about assessment as something that we the *teachers* do. Or to put it another way, the students do the work and then wait for the teacher to tell them if they "got it right."

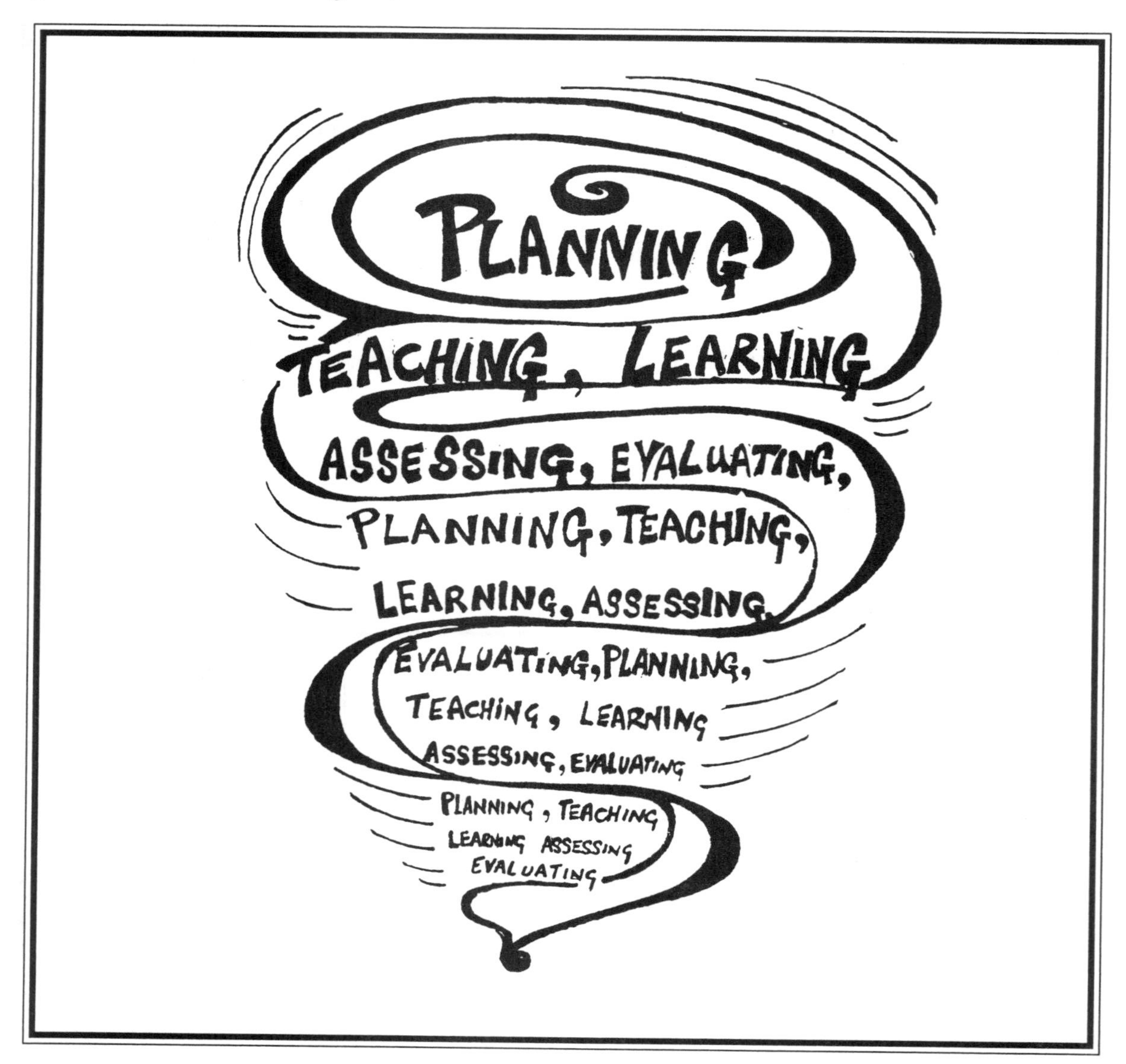

Reality Check!

We might be assessing the learning. We might think we have to because that's our job. Isn't that what teachers do?

The point is, we shouldn't be the only ones doing it.

Learners need to learn how to assess their own learning, and we should be increasingly handing over to them more and more responsibility for this.

This misconception is a particularly dangerous one. A lot of power comes with assessment, and sometimes we as teachers are tempted to hold on to this power. It's rather nice being the Expert and Ruler and Chief Judge in your own classroom kingdom, isn't it?

The trouble is, the more we hang on to this power, the less empowered we make our learners.

The more a learner has to wait to get approval or the OK from someone else–be it a parent, a teacher or any other authority figure–the less the learner is likely to become an independent, self-regulating, self-disciplined, self-critical, self-loving, self-motivated, self-developing, empowered, community-enriching member of our society.

If we perpetually make our students dependent for their validation on us, chances are they will end up as adults who don't know how to value themselves (or to trust their own validations). They will be constantly seeking and desperately needing validation from everyone–their partners, their families, their friends, their employers, and even the government! In other words, in holding on to this power over assessment, we are teaching our students how to become dependent and de-powered for the rest of their lives.

Now, this is a major, far-reaching claim we're making here. But why is it, for example, that the number one best-sellers in the United States today tend to be self-help books–books in which the authors step in to tell us (like a parent/teacher/doctor/authority figure) how to straighten out our lives? And what do the best of these do? They tell us, as adults, how to tell ourselves we're really OK!

But there is another, more selfish, reason for debunking this misconception–and that is teacher survival! The more obsessed with assessment our society becomes, the more neurotic everyone becomes about having to "check" the learning–and that means more and more unproductive time for teachers that would be better spent on the facilitating of learning. The more we can involve our students in the assessment of their own learning, and the more collaborative we can make this business, the more time we will have to devote to our students' real learning needs.

Misconception number 3

(This is really another version of Misconception number 2.) We tend to think of assessment as something that is done *to* the learner.

Reality Check!

In fact, good assessment is something the learners do to themselves, too. It's also something teachers do to themselves–we assess the learning *and* assess our teaching.

Misconception number 4

We tend to think assessment involves measurement, and this usually means assigning to the learning a numerical or alphabetical mark or grade.

Reality Check!

Measurement is really just a systematized and abstract form of description. For example, we describe height, length, weight, etc. by providing a measurement on a particular scale. When we give a person's height, we know by convention that we are referring only to the distance from the top of the head to the soles of the feet. We're not describing or implying anything else about the person. It is a one-dimensional scale.

Consider Jenny and Billy

Jenny has written a story.	Billy has written a story.
Jenny's spelling is wonderfully accurate throughout.	Billy has spelling mistakes all over the place!
Jenny's handwriting is neat and perfectly legible.	Billy's handwriting is a scrawl and a torment to the eyes!
Jenny's story has a predictable beginning, middle, and end, just like the teacher's example.	Billy's story is structuralily quite unusual–he's tried to use a flashback device, and it really makes the reader think.
Jenny's story is rather boring because it is very much like everyone else's.	Billy's story is highly imaginative. His ideas are obviously his own, and he makes the reader want to read on.
What grade, on an *A, B, C, D, (Fail)* scale, do you give Jenny?	What grade, on an *A, B, C, D, (Fail)* scale, do you give Billy?

When we resort to numbers or letter grades to describe or assess learning, we are metaphorically drawing on these other measurement scales. The trouble is, they don't match with learning because it is not a one-dimensional process. Learning is dynamic and multifaceted, and any attempt to reduce it to one dimension is going to end up ambiguous and misleading–or worse, meaningless.

The one-dimensional scale just doesn't work, does it? You might end up by giving Jenny a *B* because she is accurate and neat but too boring to be an *A*, while Billy gets a *B* because he's imaginative and innovative but far too sloppy with his spelling and presentation to warrant an *A*. So both might get *B*'s, but one is really quite different from the other. The one-dimensional scale doesn't tell us or the learner (or the parent, for that matter) anything useful about the learning.

Any system we invent as teachers to describe learning should first and foremost meet these criteria. Does it help the learner, and us, understand:

- **what they know and need to know *(Knowledge and Understanding)*;**
- **what they can do and need to be able to do *(Skills and Strategies)*; and**
- **what they know and can do so they can know and do it better *(Attitudes and Values)*.**

Misconception number 5

We tend to think of learning as a kind of assembly-line or one-track, single-direction, linear trajectory or progression. And as a result of this assembly-line metaphor, we tend to see assessment as the process of finding out how far along that trajectory or assembly line the learner has progressed.

We have two special people in particular to thank for this:

(a) Henry Ford, the Patron Saint of the Factory System and proud Founding Father of the assembly line; and (b) B. F. Skinner, who liked to reduce all learning interaction to nice, simplistic, one-way, linear stimulus/response equations like **S → R.**

Reality Check!

This is a very dangerous misconception, too, because it can be pervasive and subliminal–we don't even know we're thinking like this!

Look at what we do. We arrange our schools in a series of ascending "grades." (Isn't that just another assembly line?) We classify textbooks and reading material according to "grade level." We debate whether to "promote" students (i.e., move them along the assembly line). We call assessing children's work "grading" (i.e., determining where to place it on this ascending, single-track scale). We talk about "graduating"–meaning that the learner has come through the gradients of learning. We have "undergraduates," who haven't yet made the grade. And yes, we talk about making the grade!

We remember Henry Ford for the Model T. But doesn't this assembly-line thinking give us Model T learners–all built from the same learning parts to the same learning specifications with the same learning conditions? And most frightening of all, *do we expect them all to perform the same, too?*

Isn't this the country that, above all else, values individual freedom and the right to be different and to make your own way in the world?

Henry Ford's assembly-line ideas might have made a tremendous contribution to the American economy of his day, but schools are not learning factories, and children are not incomplete and inert products sitting on an assembly line, passively waiting for us to bolt on the next bit of learning machinery.

Nor does learning growth follow the same pathway or single-direction, one-track, linear trajectory of an assembly line or Skinner's stimulus-and-response bows and arrows. Learning will likely take many divergent paths. And it might differ with cultural background, individual makeup (ability, temperament, health, and experience), and the learner's compatibility with the teacher and the learning environment. Nor will it be a smooth, predictable incline. Learning often comes in fits and starts; there are plateaus where nothing seems to happen, and sudden, inexplicable accelerations.

Misconception number 6

We tend to think about learning in the same way and with the same language and expectations we use when we think about our two great national pastimes: sports and business. It's all about winning or losing, about success or failure, about getting rich or going broke.

Reality Check!

Like Henry Ford's assembly line, we owe this misconception to the power of popular metaphors, because that's what sports and business are in this little mind deception–unhelpful metaphors.

Learning is much more subtle than a baseball game (sorry, sports fans). In baseball, you go for home runs; but in learning, there are no home runs, because the game never ends and you never run out of bases–you just get to one base and then set out for the next, and the next, and the next . . .

Learning is far more multifaceted than business, too. In business you measure your success by how much capital or money you have (or owe!). In learning we have a kind of capital in the form of our accumulated experience. But while in business we can use up our capital and go broke, the learner never does, because the more we use our experience, the more we learn.

Thinking about learning in terms of winners or losers and success or failure is dangerous and deceptive for another reason–because it really is an extension of binary thinking.

Binary thinking is the kind of erroneous mind-set that conditions us to believe that for every question or situation or issue there are only two possibilities: right/wrong, yes/no, good/bad, etc.

This binary thinking can show up in nearly every area of our lives–in politics (Republican or Democrat, liberal or conservative, communist or capitalist, right wing or left wing), in gender (men versus women), in race (us and them), in justice (guilty or not guilty, the prosecution versus the defense), and in religion and theology (good or evil, right or wrong, heaven or hell). Sadly, binary thinking surfaces in education, too–

answers are either right or wrong, children pass or fail, and we have mainstream education and special education.

Of course, for some things, binary thinking is appropriate. Our computers, for instance, wouldn't exist without it. But most important issues are far too complex to be simplified in this way. Especially people issues.

Misconception number 7

We tend to think assessment is something you do by "testing."

This is a BIG misconception, and it is pervasive. We have teacher-made tests, schoolwide tests, publishers' tests, standardized tests, state-mandated tests–in fact, we have a test industry!

Reality Check!

What is a test, really? It is an attempt to artificially simulate the behavior you want to measure. For example, in a reading test, instead of doing real reading (or authentic reading), we try to make the learners do the kinds of things they would have to do in real authentic reading, to see if they can do them.

There are four *How* questions (at least) that we ought to ask before deciding to use a test.

1. **How valid is this test?**
   Is the artificially simulated behavior the same or similar to the real behavior we're trying to measure? The trouble with a lot of testing is that we tend to end up testing that which is testable, and leaving out a lot of significant "stuff" because we just can't readily "test" it–things like attitude, motivation, and creativity.

2. **How reliable is the test?**
   The problem with artificially simulated behavior is that we don't know how typical it is. Is this how the learner would normally respond, or is the child low on energy today, maybe coming down with a cold or some debilitating illness? Or maybe the child had a bad experience at home that is making him or her depressed and low in motivation for the task.

3. **How useful is the test to the learner and the one who is supposed to be facilitating the learning–the teacher?**
   We need to ask how the test is going to make the instruction more effective and how it will enhance the learning.

4. **How necessary is the test?**
   Why rely on artificially simulated behavior when, much of the time, we can observe and evaluate the real or "authentic" behavior itself? For example, why test reading with artificial reading tests when we can hear and observe children reading any day of the week in our own classrooms? Why test spelling by dictating words from a teacher or test publisher's list when surely the real test of how well the students spell can be found in their writing? Much of the time the answers to our assessment questions are right there in our classrooms, under our noses. To take advantage of these assessment opportunities, we need other procedures and strategies besides the habitual test–and that is what Chapter 4 is all about!

Testing the Test

The following are some of the major criticisms made about traditional standardized tests and the way they have been used:

- **Testing takes time away from instruction and learning.**
- **Most standardized tests are used for group description and categorization, not for individual diagnostic purposes.**
- **Testing does not assist the instruction or learning in any direct or obvious way.**
- **Testing might distort or even hijack the instruction, especially when teachers feel compelled to teach to the test.**
- **Test results do not tell students anything they can use in their own learning, nor do they tell teachers anything they can use in any specific way in their instruction. Furthermore, they do not tell parents anything they can use to participate in the learning process.**
- **Tests provide a snapshot of the student's knowledge and skills at a specific point in time, but they do not give us information on how the learner arrived at that point or what learning processes the learner is using.**
- **Tests compare a student's progress with a statistical norm, while for instruction we need to compare a student's current learning with the student's own previous learning.**
- **Test results are frequently misunderstood and misinterpreted–that's because the results are reported in numerical or alphabetical codes that need skilled and sophisticated interpretation.**
- **Test results might discourage collaboration between students and teachers, because the single-score result tends to pitch student against student, and even teacher against teacher and school against school.**
- **Testing is expensive, not only because of the time it takes (paid teacher time), but also the cost of materials and personnel to administer and score the tests. (All of the assessment procedures discussed in this book are teacher-made, and in that sense, they are "free.")**

Of course there are times when simulated behavior is a necessary and indeed, preferred option. For example, it is better for pilots to learn to land a large airliner at Kennedy International Airport using a flight simulator rather than letting them practice with a real aircraft filled with real passengers! But in our classrooms, for the most part, it is better and easier for students to practice learning in authentic situations and to have that learning assessed in simple, authentic ways.

Misconception number 8

We seem to believe that assessment requires us to *classify* or *label* children. In particular, we label some children as "disabled." Some students are given an even narrower title: we label them as "learning disabled." Labeling children as "learning disabled" makes our job easier because the label lets us off the hook. It's not *our* fault that they can't learn–it's *their* fault. They're just *that* kind of children! They're learning disabled, and by definition, learning disabled children don't learn!

Reality Check!

When we think about it, isn't this labeling just plain repugnant? Sure, helping some children learn is a challenge, but when we talk (and think) about a child as being disabled, we concentrate on all the things that child cannot do and ignore all the things the child is able to do. As a result, instead of seeing the child, we see only the disability.

We get very precise with these classifications, too. For example, in traditional classrooms it is very common to classify a child as having ADD. Studies of these children often reveal that this dysfunction might be responsible for as little as 10 percent of the child's total behavior. Yet once a child is classified in this way ("Oh, he's my ADD kid . . ."), everything that is done for the child seems to be modified by, and influenced by, that 10 percent! Isn't this a classic case of the tail wagging the dog?

What is worse, these labels stick. They set up expectations (usually low ones), and expectations have a nasty habit of becoming self-fulfilling prophecies. These labels can hurt, too. Sadly, one of the most disabling things we can do to a child is to label him or her *disabled*. We can do this with the best of intentions. (People said that about corporal punishment and even slavery!) We might do it because that is the way we have been trained. (In which case, we must retrain!) We might do it out of a compulsive need for classificatory tidiness. (In which case, we might need professional help!) We might even do it in order to secure funding. And if that's the case, we must change the systems and the way our community thinks. The fact is, none of these reasons is a good reason to label a child.

> ***Labeling as an assessment strategy is only good for assessing fossils–because fossils don't change. Learners do change. Good learners transform themselves all the time. Good teachers help make those transformations happen. Labeling merely fixes immature learners in a learning time warp forever.***

Misconception number 9

Somewhere–written in the stars, perhaps–is the "right" way to do this assessment business. And when we have discovered it, then all we will have to do is make sure all the teachers do the same thing and we will not need to worry about assessment ever again!

Reality check!

Every learning interaction is highly complex and, therefore, unique. Whatever system works for one teacher or for one group of teachers and learners, will not necessarily be perfect for another group.

Of course, we need to be systematic and consistent, and that means we are going to need assessment systems and procedures. But that doesn't mean they have to provide "templates" that teachers will then follow with robotic mindlessness.

How Did All These Misconceptions Come About?

The main reason for all these misconceptions is that over time, as we've come to look more closely at our assessment needs, our ideas on the best way to do assessment have changed.

Once Upon an Assessment Time: A Brief History of Assessment Beliefs and Practices

Chapter One

Once upon a time (about a generation ago), the thinking on assessment was fairly unanimous–the best way, the right way, the only way to get a clear picture as to whether children had learned what they were supposed to have learned was to give them a **TEST**. Preferably a "scientifically standardized test." If it was **"SCIENTIFIC,"** it was good. One might not have understood the methodology or known how to interpret the results soundly, but because it was scientific, it just had to be right. Otherwise, it wouldn't be scientific, would it?

'Course, the people making the tests didn't mind, because this was turning into a big business, and I mean **BIG!**

Chapter Two

But there were critics in that far-off land, and in time their voices began to be heard.

"Someone ought to look more closely at this unquestioning acceptance of standardized tests as the ultimate and often sole measure of attainment!" they declared. Of course, that "someone" wasn't listening, or at least was not answering the phone.

But this didn't put the critics off. They went right on criticizing, which is what critics do best. They pointed out that these big testing rodeos seemed to stir up a lot of dust but didn't seem to help the teachers teach any better.

"We kind of thought that was the main point," they said.

Of course, people treated this idea with the kind of contempt they thought it deserved. Especially the test makers.

The critics also pointed out that these testing festivities seemed to take up a heck of a lot of good teaching time–and that sometimes teachers were so afraid of the testing festivities that they would forget about all the other important things the children were supposed to be learning and only teach things that were in the tests.

There were some children who didn't seem to be able to do the tests, anyway, because they didn't speak English very well. And some children had one of those quirky things called an imagination, so when it came to choosing the "right" answer from a list of choices, they tended to choose quirky wrong answers–which they could have justified if someone had bothered to ask them. But of course, no one ever did.

The critics also pointed out that these tests just gave a snapshot, but what teachers needed was a whole lot of snapshots, so they could see how the learning was going over a period of time. All the test people said was, "Then do more testing!" But this didn't please the critics, either, because what they really wanted to do was do more teaching!

As time went on, teachers began to listen to the critics and, being in the learning business, they did a bit of learning about all this themselves.

"All right!" said the teachers. "Fair enough! But how else are we going to assess children's learning?"

Chapter Three

No one quite knew the answer to that question, until one day a wise old teacher suddenly jumped out of her bath and ran through the streets in her bathrobe, shouting, **"Eureka!"** (Which was nudist bathing for, "I have it!")

"Instead of tests, we'll rely on our own observations of what children do while they're learning!" she said.

Now all the other teachers were delighted and enraptured by this idea. After all, they were already good at this because they did it all the time as part of their classroom instruction. All they had to do was to be a little more methodical and systematic about it and, in particular, take notes when they saw something significant and keep anecdotal records.

Kidwatching was born!

Of course, some teachers didn't want to call it *kidwatching*, so they called it other things, like **Observational Assessment**, because that's what you did, or **Authentic Assessment**, because it involved looking at authentic learning in natural or authentic settings. Some teachers who had been to the music festival at Woodstock wanted to call it **Alternative Assessment**, but others said that was a bit silly if they hoped that one day it would be the mainstream way of assessing learning.

Chapter Four

But even this didn't silence all the critics.

"This observational assessment is all very well, but you don't have anything to prove that what you say you've observed is really happening!" the critics said. "Where's your data? Where's your proof?"

"Hmmmmmm!" said the teachers thoughtfully. "Then maybe we should keep samples of the children's work in order to show what they can do." So they did this, and they put the samples into special folders, which they called "portfolios"–and **Portfolio Assessment** was born!

Chapter Five

Portfolios sprang up all over the land. Teachers found they could ask the children to help them choose pieces to go into their portfolio. This made the children excited, too, because they felt like they were part of the assessment process. Portfolios began to get fatter and fatter as more and more stuff was crammed into them.

Then the critics popped out again from under their educational bridges.

"Wait a minute!" they said. "Those portfolios are becoming great compost heaps of stuff, but do they really give a clear and accurate picture of what a child has learned or needs to learn? We think not! And what's more, they don't give us any idea how far along the learning journey each child is. And since each portfolio seems to be different, how can you compare one class with another class, or one school with another school? And if you can't do that, how can you be sure the teachers are doing a good job and deserve all the money we're paying them?"

Meanwhile, the people began to feel more and more insecure and confused by all these arguments. And whenever people feel insecure about something, they tend to fall back on what they know or what happened to them. So they began to say, "Do we really need these new-fangled things? Why can't we just have a test like we used to have?"

This caused random outbreaks of nostalgia, and whenever you have confusion and outbreaks of nostalgia, you usually find politicians.

Sure enough, as soon as some people began talking like this, up jumped the politicians, and they said, "We can do better than test–we'll devise a **Super Test!** We'll give our test to everyone in the land, and then we'll know everything we need to know and we'll be able to get rid of the useless teachers and have more money to spend on useful things like city halls and bigger limousines for politicians to drive around in."

Chapter Six

The teachers were depressed when they heard this. "Aren't we ever going to get to live happily ever after like the heroes in fairy tales?" they asked.

And the critics said, "Probably not, but keep working on it."

So they did . . .

And that's why, instead of this story ending with those time-honored words *THE END*, it concludes with *TO BE CONTINUED* . . .

From Kidwatching to Portfolios

Originally a portfolio was a folder kept by artists in which they might put samples of their work to show to a gallery or a potential buyer. Artists sometimes kept portfolios for themselves, too–folders containing works in progress or sketches or ideas that needed further development.

Portfolios are often described or talked about as an assessment method, but that is rather misleading. In fact, the portfolio itself is just a receptacle, or container. The assessment lies in the process by which it is created. This can involve a range of valuable assessment strategies. First, the learning artifacts are selected on the basis of some form of criteria (by the student or the teacher, or both). This selection process might develop as a result of student and teacher reflection; the portfolio might be organized to give a particular view of the learning; its contents could be cataloged or categorized and classified to highlight particular aspects of the learning. They might be dated to enable learning to be viewed over time, and they might include anecdotal notes and explanations to provide further insight into the process and purpose of the learning.

Portfolios have received a wide degree of acceptance in many parts of the United States–but their development has been in no way consistent or uniform. And while they have their strengths, they also have their weaknesses. (To make it even more confusing, often their strengths are also their weaknesses!)

Are Portfolios Enough?

One of the major difficulties schools have with portfolios is how to reconcile what seems to be the conflicting assessment needs of teachers and the assessment needs of administrators and the wider taxpaying community.

On the one hand, teachers argue passionately that assessment needs to serve, and be part of, their instruction. They criticize testing programs because they interrupt, or disrupt, or even–when teachers try to "teach to the test"–distort the classroom instruction. Teachers have seized on portfolios because they see them as more organic vehicles for assessment. The portfolios grow out of, and relate to, the instruction. They can be used to reflect the whole range of the curriculum in an integrated way. They provide a much more comprehensive and over-time picture of the learner and the learning. And because the students can also be involved in the portfolio assessment process, they feel a greater sense of ownership–certainly more than they might have felt about a set of test scores.

Furthermore, rather than encouraging students to compare themselves with other students' achievements and learning curve, the portfolio encourages students to compare their current learning with their own past learning, resulting in a greater sense of empowerment and responsibility for their own knowledge. The learning is more meaningful to students and their parents because it is displayed as real artifacts rather than sets of abstract numbers or numerical letter or number grades. Telling a parent that a child is a B+, or scored 67%, or is on the ninth percentile, tells them nothing about what their child knows or can do. But the student's own learning logs and work samples chosen over time show not only where the child is now but how he or she came to this point.

On the other hand, administrators and people in other sectors of the community–particularly organized groups of taxpayers–are often more interested in administrative and accountability issues. They want information that will help them provide appropriate resources and plan for future resource and personnel needs. They also want information that will provide answers to questions such as: Are the children learning? Are the teachers doing their job? Are schools doing their job? Administrators don't want to wade through piles of portfolios, no matter how vivid and interesting the material inside, because they provide *too much* information, and information that is too diverse. They don't need to see each child as a unique, individual learner. They need summaries and group profiles, information that enables them to compare and contrast, to average and compute. They want trends and generalizations, not the specifics and the minutiae of classroom learning.

So, to answer the question: "Are portfolios enough?" The answer must be "No," because they do not meet all our assessment needs. But if that is the case, we also need to ask the question: "Is there any way we are going to be able to resolve these issues of assessment for instruction versus assessment for administrative and accountability needs?"

The answer is "Yes"–in fact, that is the key purpose of this book!

But first we have to make some fundamental changes to some prevailing mind-sets when it comes to assessment!

Assessment Mind-Sets We Need to Change

1. We must stop trying to find a "test substitute," or a signle, one and only "alternative" to the traditional standardized test.

Many teachers have tended to use portfolios as test substitutes. Everything else they happened to do in the classroom tended to be the same, but instead of ending up with a pile of test papers to put in a test file, they ended up with a pile of miscellaneous pieces of work that they put in a portfolio.

Portfolios are not like tests. They have different strengths and do different things, and it is important that we recognize what these are and use them where they are most effective.

Perhaps as a result of this "test substitute" mind-set, in some parts of the country there have been many attempts to try to make portfolios act even more like standardized tests. Teachers and administrators have tried to standardize certain aspects of the portfolios, especially their content and organization.

They might also require certain items that have more of a standardized test feel about them. For example, in some districts, students are given experiences with specific reading texts, and their responses are assessed according to standardized criteria. Such procedures might be more reliable, and the texts chosen might be more authentic than the traditional test material, but it's still an artificial process and one that interrupts or sits apart from the learning. The logistics of these procedures are often time-consuming and expensive to implement. The resulting portfolio becomes a kind of hybrid and, as with most compromises, doesn't really satisfy either of the parties.

So what do we do about this mind-set? When we think in the test mode, we start looking for one instrument or vehicle that will provide the answer to all our assessment needs. But if we change our thinking about these things and instead look at assessment as an organic part of the learning process, then we don't have to rely on one answer to our assessment questions. Instead, as we will see in later chapters, we can draw on a whole exciting repertoire of assessment strategies and tools. These include portfolios, along with many other procedures. (And yes, we can even include tests in there if we choose!)

> ***2. We must give first priority to the assessment of individual learning and then extract the more generalized assessment information needed for administrative and accountability purposes from that–not the other way around.***

With traditional testing, we tend to use group and whole population assessment procedures to make decisions about what is appropriate instruction for individual learners. We find out the general and apply it to the specific.

In particular, we tend to judge the learning of an individual by comparing it with hypothetical mathematical constructs like the norm, or the average, or the grade level.

Now, statistical norms might have their statistical uses. Among other things, they help administrators quantify resource needs and determine how much money they need from their political masters. But a statistical norm is a hypothetical property of a group of numbers, not a living, learning human being. It doesn't tell us what a child knows or can do or how a child feels about learning–all things we need to know in order to plan effective instruction. In particular, referencing our instruction to a statistical norm shortchanges both our so-called "gifted" students (because it tends to make us lower our expectations) and those students at the other end of the spectrum (because we tend to pitch and pace the learning inappropriately).

The best benchmark for measuring a student's learning is not a "norm" or a "test score" or a "grade level," but rather the student's learning to date. That is why assessment needs to be organic–because it enables us to constantly re-gear the instruction to the learning.

Our main task as educators is to facilitate learning; therefore, the chief assessment priority must be the continuous learning-facilitating assessment of the individual learner. Sure, teachers need classrooms and resources and personnel to assist and support them, and someone has to plan and pay for all that. We need assessment for these purposes, too, but if we use the group assessment measures for individual instructional purposes, we end up with imprecise caricatures of real children.

> ***3. We have to stop thinking about assessment as something we all have to do in the same way and at the same point in time!***

We had to think about assessment that way with the standardized test because that was part of its standardization, but we don't have to do that with organic assessment because we will be using a range of strategies and assessment tools–whatever is appropriate for the learning: and because our assessment will be continuous–we'll be doing it all the time, not in one dramatic, time-consuming, learning-interrupting bout of assessment.

It is true that assessment for administrative and accountability purposes tends to be asked for at one particular point in time. That's understandable because that information is needed for forward planning, resource buying, budgeting, etc. And those things have to be done at particular times in the year.

But that is assessment *reporting*! We need to make a clear distinction in our minds between assessment *making*–which should be an organic part of the instruction and continuous throughout the year–and assessment *reporting*, which we do for critical administrative and accountability purposes.

> ***4. What we wish to show in this book is that we can have it all! We can do continuous organic assessment based on authentic learning experiences that will inform and enrich the learning in our classrooms, AND at the same time accumulate assessment records that can provide the kind of assessment snapshot and statistical summary administrators need for planning and accountability purposes. Yes, we can have our assessment cake and eat it, too! What's more, it won't take any extra time (well, hardly any) because the mathematical fancy footwork is very simple, and if you are using a computer to store your Learning Assessment Record (the document that we will be using to summarize our learning assessments), it can all be done by the machine in the blink of an eye.***

So, What Do We Really Want from Our Assessment System?

Before beginning to design this system that is going to take advantage of all the breakthroughs and merits of current systems and also avoid or minimize their defects, we should draw up a shopping list, noting the criteria that we need to apply:

It will need to be **organic**–that is, we want what we do for assessment to be an integral part of the instruction.

We want it to be **authentic**–in other words, we want it to relate to learning in a first-hand way.

We want it to be **practical** and easy to do–it should be easy to operate; we don't want to waste a lot of valuable teaching time setting it up and making it work.

We want it to be **simple**–we don't want it to be simplistic, but we *do* want something that everyone–students, teachers, parents, and administrators–will understand and appreciate.

We want it to be **motivational** for teachers and learners–in other words, we want it to give positive feedback to teachers and learners, to help them set high goals and inspire them to give it their best shot.

We want it to be as **positive** as possible–we want the main focus to be on what the learners know, what they can do, and what they believe.

We want it to be **collaborative**–to involve in an inclusive and participatory way, not just the teacher, but also, wherever possible, the learners, the parents, the class, the school administrators, and the community.

We want it to be appropriately **informative**–to tell the learners, the teachers, the parents, the school administrators, and the district administrators what they need to know in order to do their jobs properly.

We want it to be **systematic**–the process should be appropriately structured and well-organized so that it unfolds easily and efficiently, and without glitches or mishaps.

We want it to meet **both** the **instructional classroom needs** and **administrative and accountability needs**–in that order of importance.

Now, that's a tall order! So, how do we begin?

We Do It In Four Easy Steps

Step 1: We do an Assessment Audit. (We talk about how to do this in Chapter 2.)

Step 2: We prepare a Learning Assessment Plan and sort out our assessment strategies and tools. Our Learning Assessment Plan then becomes our Learning Assessment Record in which we will be able to record summaries of our students' learning. (We talk about how to do the learning part in Chapter 3 and the assessment strategizing part in Chapter 4.)

Step 3: Then we do a Learning Assessment Schedule for the year, just to prompt us and make sure we put our plans into action. (We talk about this in Chapter 5.)

Step 4: Then we **start teaching** and, from time to time, we use the Learning Assessment Record to do a survey of the student population so our administrators can get an overview of the learning in the grades or the school or the school district. (In Chapter 6, we show you how this happens, and in Chapter 7, in case Murphy's Law starts to operate, we talk about potential problems and things that might go wrong, and how to fix them.)

"But wait! I'm only a classroom teacher! Can I do this all by myself?"

In the past, assessment has tended to be one of those things that has been decided upon from on high. Often what happens is that someone in authority goes to a conference or hears what some other school is doing and decides that "everyone else around here is going to do that, too!"

When it happens like that, the classroom teachers tend to shrug their shoulders, get on with their teaching, and do what the "powers that be" declare they *should* do about assessment. With so little ownership, it's no wonder teachers often feel unmotivated and turned off by assessment issues!

One of the major strengths of the organic learning assessment system outlined in this book is that it can be used at all levels of the school community.

This Is an Adaptable and Inclusive Approach to Learning Assessment

So, what does that mean? Well, you can use the organic learning assessment system in a number of different ways, and you can use it alongside, and together with, other assessment requirements and systems.

Individual classroom teachers, all on their own, can follow the procedures in this book to prepare an organic Learning Assessment Plan for the students in their classrooms.

OR

A group of teachers within a school can arrange to meet and work together to develop their own collaborative Learning Assessment Plan for their students.

OR

An entire school faculty can work together to prepare a schoolwide Learning Assessment Plan for all of the students in their particular school.

OR

A whole district can bring representatives together from the different member schools to plan and develop a districwide Learning Assessment Plan.

OR

An entire state or country can embark on this kind of exercise!
(Hallelujah!)

Question: What if the school or district or state already has established assessment requirements, such as a state mastery test, or a schoolwide testing program? Does this mean I can't develop a Learning Assessment Plan for my class or for our school?

Answer: No, mandated requirements do not preclude the development of a Learning Assessment Plan for a single classroom or a single school. These plans are inclusive and adaptable and are always tailor-made to meet local needs and conditions. Just go through the procedures that include the state or school requirements as part of the plan.

Right! So, now you've made your way through Chapter 1! Time for a little "test" to check on your "assessmentality."

Chapter Review: Multiple-Choice Nightmares

In order to review your thinking as a result of reading this first chapter, please complete the following statements, choosing the correct, or most likely, answer in each case.

1. Standardized tests used to be used extensively because
   (a) they were all the same height.
   (b) you could scientifically rig the results.
   (c) you were more likely to get one in your size.
   (d) they enabled you to tell the parents their children were hopeless without getting sued.

2. The best way to get good results on a multiple-choice test is to
   (a) use a multiple-choice typewriter.
   (b) start from the top.
   (c) copy somebody else's answers.
   (d) mark it yourself.

3. Evaluation is
   (a) a speech impediment brought on by the malformation of the uvula.
   (b) that which comes after D-valuation and before F-valuation.
   (c) the process of crossing a valley.
   (d) the opposite of adamluation.

4. You would be likely to find alternative assessment being used
   (a) in an operating theater when the surgeon has just realized he's taken off the wrong leg.
   (b) when you're applying to live in a hippie commune.
   (c) when you're deciding to get married for the second time.
   (d) when you're trying to decide where to go for lunch.

5. Who invented Organic Assessment?
   (a) Greenpeace
   (b) Harold Wurlitzer
   (c) Bela Lugosi
   (d) Christian Barnard

6. The main point made in this chapter is that
   (a) assessment assessment needs further assessment.
   (b) no matter what you do for assessment, you won't get no satisfaction.
   (c) *your* assessment is all right–it's everyone else's that's wrong.
   (d) there is no main point.

Chapter 2

Getting Focused

Who Are We Doing This For?

In This Chapter

- Time to Get Set Up
- But What If You Have to Do This On Your Own?
- First We Need an Assessment Audit
- So, How Do We Do This Assessment Audit?
- Assessment Audit Example
- After the *Why* Questions Come the *How* Questions
- Chapter Review: A True-Or-False Test

Time to Get Set Up

Before we can begin the nitty-gritty of our assessment planning, there are a number of "setting up" tasks we need to do. These will take a little time (and patience!) and are best done collaboratively, which means getting a consensus of opinion on some important professional issues–and getting *that* might take even more time! But the important thing about this approach to assessment is that once we have done the basic planning, it will take very little maintenance to keep it up and running.

Working collaboratively might take a little administrative ingenuity, too, but there are distinct advantages:

- You share the planning load.
- You benefit from everyone else's experiences.
- You get to say what you actually think–and you might be surprised to find you don't always think what you thought you thought!
- Everyone who participates also shares in the ownership of the plan you devise.
- Setting up collaboratively means you and your colleagues will take an interest in what's happening in each other's classrooms, so everyone will be motivated to make the plan work.

But What If You Have to Do This On Your Own?

It might be that your colleagues are just not ready for this approach. Maybe they're happy doing things the way they've always done them, regardless of any argument or attempts on your part to get some fresh philosophical blood moving in their tired old veins. Never mind–you can still do all this in your classroom all by yourself. And who knows, the excitement you generate might be just the thing those other teachers need to get them thinking. Although you might be on your own this year, it could be that next year, you'll be leading your colleagues down the same assessment highway!

First We Need an Assessment Audit

We need to do an Assessment Audit to find answers to three key questions:

1. **Who are we doing this for?**
   We need to begin by deciding who our "stakeholders" are. Stakeholders will vary somewhat from class to class, school to school, and district to district; but they will almost certainly include our students and their parents and families, our school administrators and district officials, and, of course, ourselves–the teachers. Other stakeholders might include consultants, researchers, our local university, sponsors and benefactors, and the taxpaying community.

2. **What do they need the information for?**
   We need to ask this question because different stakeholders might have different purposes.

3. **What kind of information do they need?**
   When we have a clear idea of what kind of assessment information we are going to be expected to provide, we can start thinking about how we are going to get that information. And once we've solved that, we can start thinking about how we are going to present the information to our various stakeholders so that it is: (a) meaningful–i.e., so our stakeholders can understand it!; and (b) so everyone can use it positively–i.e., to help our learners learn more, and learn more effectively.

   That's the plan of action we have to follow to get the first part of this assessment gig on the road!

So, How Do We Do This Assessment Audit?

First, we should read the rest of this book so we know where all this is heading! Then we should gather together as many of the participants as possible–or at least a suitably representative group–and brainstorm until we have gathered all the information we need.

Of course, if you are a teacher doing this on your own for your own class, you'll probably have to brainstorm all by yourself. (But at least you won't have to deal with any differences of opinion!)

Make up a chart like the one on this page on an overhead transparency, or on large sheets of paper, and write down your answers as you go.

Sample Assessment Audit Form

Assessment Audit

For:* ______________________________

Who are we doing this learning assessment for?	What do they need the information for? *(Notes can begin with the words, "So they can…")*	What kind of information do they need? *(Notes can begin with the words, "They need…")*

****My class, or our school, or our school district***

Assessment Audit Example

The following is an example of what a completed Assessment Audit might look like.

Assessment Audit

For: <u>My grade 3 class</u>

Who are we doing this learning assessment for?	What do they need the information for?	What kind of information do they need?
My students	• So they can feel good about their own learning. • So they feel they are making progress with their own learning. • So they know what they can do and what they need to work at. • So they can begin to take more responsibility for what they are learning. • So they can internalize the assessment process and use it to monitor and develop their own learning. • So they can set some goals for themselves, and in the process learn about goal-setting.	• They need oral feedback about their work–not always answers but questions, too–things they need in order to come to terms with themselves. • They need written comments that make specific points about their work–not numbers or letter grades! • Don't be so critical that they become discouraged–keep it positive, but challenging. Keep pushing back that learning frontier! • They need models of work by other children and by the teacher to give them a full sense of the process, some ideas as to standards of work expected, and motivation to strive even harder. • They need their own assessments, too–and those of their peers and their parents–so they can use them as a frame of reference.
The students' parents and families	• So they can share and participate in the student's learning. • So they can help appropriately with homework. • So they can give appropriate encouragement and help with motivation.	• They need conference time feedback on how their child is progressing, with examples from the child's portfolio. This should happen at least twice a year and more often if there is a problem.

Assessment Audit

For: My grade 3 class

Who are we doing this learning assessment for?	**What do they need the information for?**	**What kind of information do they need?**
The students' parents and families *(continued)*		• They need written reports that tell them, in some detail and with appropriate narrative, what their child has learned and what he or she is in the process of learning. • They need to see samples of the child's work so they can see what he or she is doing and have opportunities to talk with the child about the work.
Principal	• So he or she can plan ahead and buy the resources the school needs. • So the principal can be sure my class is meeting the school's learning goals. • To determine whether I am doing a good job managing the class and managing the learning. • So he or she can be sure the school as a whole is doing a good job and can demonstrate this to our superintendent and others.	• They need surveys that provide a snapshot of the whole class in order to ensure that I am catering to all the children. • They need surveys that give a snapshot of the content areas in order to make sure I am dealing with the whole curriculum.
Me (the teacher)	• So I know what the children know and can do, what they are starting to be able to do, and what they can't do yet–so I can plan my teaching accordingly. • So I can be sure I am teaching in a learner-centered way and meeting the learning needs of the children in my classroom. • So I can be sure I'm not overlooking anyone or spending too much time with some students and not enough time with others. • So I can be sure I am *at least* covering the whole curriculum and teaching everything I'm supposed to be teaching.	• I need descriptions of what each child in my class knows, what each child can do, and how the children feel about themselves and their learning. • I need documentation to prove that these descriptions are valid. • I need examples of work to illustrate and validate the documentation. • I need surveys of the class to meet the principal's needs and to check on the effectiveness of my own teaching.

Assessment Audit

For: <u>My grade 3 class</u>

Who are we doing this learning assessment for?	**What do they need the information for?**	**What kind of information do they need?**
Me (the teacher) *(continued)*		• I need surveys of content areas to make sure I am covering the learning goals effectively. • I need this information in such a form that I can readily communicate it appropriately and meaningfully to others–the students, the parents, the principal, etc. • I need data that will help me reflect on my own teaching and continue to grow professionally.
The school district	• So the administrators can provide us with the resources we need. • So they can be sure we're all doing a good job.	• They need surveys of student learning growth, grade by grade. • They need surveys of learning in different subject areas, grade by grade.
The community	• So they can take pride in our school. • So they will understand what we are trying to do and be supportive. • So they will help us deal effectively with our politicians!	• They need displays. • They need performances. • They need to see an exciting classroom environment when they visit.

After the *Why* Questions Come the *How* Questions!

The form on pages 35-37 shows a Class Assessment Audit–the result of an individual teacher brainstorming the assessment needs for his or her class. A *School* Assessment Audit prepared by a whole faculty working collaboratively might end up being somewhat similar–but the final product is not as important as the process. That's because the chief merit of this exercise is that it helps us focus on the reasons *why* we are doing this assessment and helps prepare us for the next step in this process, where we begin to think about and plan just *how* we are going to do it.

Chapter Review: A True-Or-False Test

Are the following statements true or false? Please answer *A, B, C,* or *D,* according to the following scale:

A – I am (a) totally convinced this is completely and absolutely true, or (b) I'm just trying to impress someone.

B – I think this is somewhat true. I mean, there are more true bits than there are not true bits.

C – I'll say this is true if you pay me.

D –I'll stake my integrity on this–it's absolutely not true! Completely false! A pack of lies!

Assessment Audits are good because:

_____ They make us focus, and that improves our vision.

_____ They don't cost much.

_____ At least we get to do them ourselves.

_____ The author says so.

_____ The principal says so.

_____ The superintendent says so.

_____ The words *assessment* and *audit* start with the letter *a.*

_____ It's cheaper than using an accountant.

_____ They make us think about the needs of each stakeholder (which, as everyone knows, is another name for a butcher).

_____ They help us think about what we're doing, even though some people think that's dangerous.

_____ They help us work with our colleagues collaboratively, which is not what normally happens around here.

Chapter 3

Getting Organized

Planning the Learning So We Can Plan the Assessment

In This Chapter

- Now It's Time to Prepare a Learning Assessment Plan
- Important Principle Number 1: Learning *and* Assessment
- Important Principle Number 2: Plan for a Grade Range Rather Than Grade by Grade
- Important Principle Number 3: Plan to Go On Planning
- Important Principle Number 4: Planning Is Only a Means to an End, Not an End In Itself!
- Defining the "Subjects," or Learning Areas
- Defining the Learning Outcomes
- Looking for Three Kinds of Learning Outcomes
- Providing for the Pre-Planning and the Ongoing Planning of Learning Outcomes
- Handy Hints to Keep In Mind When Writing Learning Outcomes
- Chapter Review: The Tired Teacher's Book Report

Now It's Time to Prepare a Learning Assessment Plan

Now that we have sharpened our focus by sorting out *who* we are doing this for and what they want the information for, we need to start work on the *how*–and we do this by means of a Learning Assessment Plan.

In this chapter, we will concentrate on the Learning Plan. In the next chapter, we'll consider how our assessment strategies can be made to fit in as an organic part of the Learning Plan. However, there are four important principles we need to keep in mind.

Important Principle Number 1: Learning *and* Assessment

Note that we are not just dealing with assessment here. This is a learning plan and an assessment plan, because they will be intertwined and each will serve the other. Assessment will be an integral part of the learning process, and will derive from the learning tasks. At the same time, the learning will be all the more effective because it will be monitored and informed by the assessment.

Important Principle Number 2: Plan for a Grade Range Rather Than Grade by Grade

When working on a Learning Assessment Plan for your class (or your school or school district), it is important to define what you expect the students to learn over an overlapping range of grades–for example, kindergarten to third grade; third grade to fifth grade; and fifth grade to eighth grade, etc.–rather than trying to define specific outcomes for each particular grade level. There are a number of reasons for this:

(a) Remember misconception number 4 in Chapter 1? All students do not learn the same things, in the same order, in the same time span, and at the same age! Yet if we plan our learning for a specific (and mythical!) grade level, we end up teaching and thinking as if our students did just that!

(b) Furthermore, learning is continuous–it doesn't come in discrete "grade-sized" packages that start with the beginning of the academic year and conclude with the end of the year. At the start of a new class

year, learning from the previous year will still require further consolidation. Likewise, at the end of the year, there will still be aspects of our students' learning that will need further development. A grade range approach allows us to plan for learning in a more continuous, and thus more appropriate, way.

(c) A major weakness with the grade by grade stepped model (as opposed to the grade range or learning continuum model) is the impact it can have on how students and teachers perceive their work. With the stepped model, at the start of each year, the children feel they have a lot to learn, and teachers feel they have a lot to teach. The "whole year's work" hovers before them! For some students and teachers, that can be intimidating, even daunting. On the other hand, as the year passes, a stepped model might encourage students and teachers to believe there is less and less to learn–only what is left in the year's (and the grade's) quota. The result might mean a lowering of expectations and a loss of challenge and momentum.

(d) Some critical learning might take a number of grades to reach maturity for all students. Planning for a grade range rather than grade by grade gives a more accurate picture of the learning. (It also saves cluttering up our learning plans with the same learning outcomes being repeated for a number of grades.)

(e) A grade range approach tends to make the planning task simpler because it is easier to locate a specific learning outcome in a range of grades than it is to try to decide on one particular grade level for it. It's also more challenging to us when we plan the instruction because it compels us to have instructional goals that extend beyond the particular grade level we are teaching.

(f) And most important of all, a grade range approach challenges teachers to provide programs that are truly learner-centered (rather than grade-centered), and that cater to all ranges of ability and all manner of cultural and life experiences.

Important Principle Number 3: Plan to Go On Planning

If the planning and the assessment and the instruction are all going to support each other in an organic way, it is important that we allow for modifications and fine-tuning of the plan as we go along. In other words, there needs to be initial planning, or pre-planning, as we map out the year; but we also need to allow for continuous re-planning as a result of the ongoing assessment of the learning and the instruction. Also, much of what we do for the pre-planning might well be prescribed for us–by the school's plans, the school district's curriculum plans, state requirements and "standards," etc. The ongoing planning is where the teachers themselves have much more control and involvement. The more they have ownership of this area, the more committed and motivated they will feel about making this program work.

Important Principle Number 4: Planning Is Only a Means to an End, Not an End In Itself!

The proof of a good plan is not how it looks, or how long it is, or how many hours you spend preparing it, but whether it helps us teach more effectively and helps our students to learn more successfully. We need to manage the planning process so that we use people's time and skills effectively and efficiently and not get hung up on excessive (or compulsive!) detail or unhelpful elaboration. Too often, planning becomes an instrument of bureaucratic control! We need to plan in order to empower teachers and students–not to assert power over them!

Defining the "Subjects," or Learning areas

We begin by preparing the first part of the Learning Assessment Plan–the learning part.

We list the main "subjects," or Learning Areas, that provide the framework for our curriculum. For example, one approach would be to list six major Learning Areas: language arts, mathematics, science, social sciences, the arts, and physical education. Next, we subdivide two of these–language arts and the arts. But curriculum frameworks will vary from district to district and state to state, so what you do will have to satisfy local and state requirements.

Defining the Learning Outcomes

Having divided the learning into Learning Areas, or subjects, the next step is to define the key things we want our students to learn. We will be able to get help with this from a number of sources. Our school or school district might have already drawn up a curriculum framework. There could be useful books and publications we might like to use. Consultants in particular subject areas can be helpful, too.

But it is important not to underestimate our own professional experience. Even when entering a learning outcome someone else has suggested, we should take care to recast it in language we understand and feel comfortable with. In particular, we should be careful to strip away any jargon that is fuzzy! (If you and your colleagues can't agree on what a particular word or phrase means, then don't use it!)

Looking for Three Kinds of Learning Outcomes

There are three kinds of learning outcomes that we should try to achieve in our instruction for each of our Learning Areas. There will be things we want our students to:

- know and understand (Knowledge and Understandings)
- be able to do (Skills and Strategies)
- feel or believe about learning and themselves as learners (Attitudes and Values).

The Learning Assessment form on Page 45 separates these functions to ensure that we think carefully about all three aspects of learning.

Providing for the Pre-Planning and Ongoing Planning of Learning Outcomes

The form also provides shaded and unshaded spaces for writing the learning outcomes.

Pre-planned learning outcomes

The unshaded spaces are for initial planning, or *pre-planning.*

If you are a classroom teacher working on your own and preparing your own Learning Assessment plan for your class, this is where, prior to or at the start of the year, you set down the Learning Outcomes you think are appropriate for your particular grade range.

If you are part of a group of teachers doing this collaboratively–for example, as a school faculty or as representatives for your school district–this is where, prior to or at the start of the year, you collaboratively set down the learning outcomes you think are appropriate for each particular grade range.

The ongoing planning of Learning Outcomes

What about the shaded portion of the form labeled "Ongoing Planning"? As all teachers know, learning is dynamic and is often surprising and unpredictable. As the year unfolds and the learning progresses, the classroom teacher will become aware of both new learning needs and new learning opportunities. For these, new goals might need to be set and new learning outcomes defined. The teacher is able to define and enter these in the shaded areas as the year progresses and the teaching/learning process develops.

When a school faculty or school district is working collaboratively on a Learning Assessment plan, this provision for pre-planning and ongoing planning allows for a subtle balance of responsibilities. On the one hand, the pre-planned learning goals mean there will be some uniformity of standards in the teaching and learning. Teachers will know what they are expected to achieve in their teaching, and administrators will have some benchmarks for determining how well they are doing their job. In other words, the pre-planning helps with both instruction and accountability.

On the other hand, the ongoing planning allows the teaching, the learning, and the assessment of the learning to be much more interactive, flexible, and challenging. Throughout the teaching year, the learning goals can be added to, extended, or refocused. Such an approach encourages teachers to be reflective practitioners, constantly evaluating and developing their professional craft.

Ongoing planning also allows individual classroom teachers a significant degree of ownership of the assessment process. They might have contributed to the pre-planned learning outcomes, but they have full responsibility for learning outcomes that arise from the ongoing planning. With ownership comes commitment, and with commitment comes better teaching and better learning.

How many learning outcomes are derived from pre-planning, and how many stem from ongoing planning? As a rough guide, it is helpful to pre-plan about 60% of the learning outcomes and thus leave space for something like 40% for ongoing planning. But feel free to experiment and see what works well for your class, school faculty, or district.

Assessment strategies and tools

We will discuss how to complete these last two columns of the form in the next chapter.

Learning Assessment Plan for the following Grade Range: _____ to _____

Learning Outcomes	Assessment Strategies	Assessment Tools
Language Arts: **Speaking**		
Knowledge and Understandings *(Knows and understands ...)*		
Skills and Strategies *(Able to...)*		
Attitudes and Values *(Feels and believes about self and learning ...)*		
Language Arts **Listening**		
Knowledge and Understandings *(Knows and understands ...)*		
Skills and Strategies		
Attitudes and Values		
Language Arts **Reading**		
Knowledge and Understandings *(Knows and understands ...)*		

Handy Hints to Keep In Mind When Writing the Learning Outcomes

Keep them simple

You are not trying to define or pin down everything you want to happen in the classroom–you won't be able to, anyway. Children are all different, and learning often unfolds in unpredictable and highly idiosyncratic ways. This is a "game plan"–and so, as in any game, when you're playing it, you try to make the plan work. But you have to be innovative and seize unexpected opportunities, too, even if they aren't a part of your original game plan!

Don't include too many learning outcomes

The number of learning outcomes you wish to feature for each subject area is arbitrary and is up to the teachers preparing the plan. But we are sampling our students' learning, not trying to present a complete global and comprehensive picture of everything inside each student's head! Restricting the number of outcomes helps teachers focus on the key learning outcomes.

So, what is a reasonable number of learning outcomes? As a rough rule of thumb, about 25 key learning outcomes per subject per grade range is a good starting point. This allows for, say, 10 Knowledge and Understandings, 10 Skills and Strategies, and five Attitudes and Values. The number of learning outcomes doesn't have to be exactly the same for each subject or even for each grade range. Of course, the task of arriving at a consensus as to which are the key outcomes for a particular subject area might involve considerable discussion, debate, and even downright argument! But that can only have a healthy impact on our teaching! The more sure we are about what we're trying to do in our classrooms, the more focused and thus the more effective we'll be as teachers.

Keep it collaborative

By working with your colleagues, you get the best of all the brains working on the plan–and since other teachers will be participating in the process, they'll also have ownership and will be motivated to make it work!

Work from the classroom up rather than head office down

When developing a Learning Assessment Plan for an entire school or a school district, the more involvement classroom teachers have in a school or district plan, the more they will feel it is their plan and the more committed they will be to making it work.

Keep all the stakeholders informed and, wherever possible, involved

While the teachers must play a key role in assessment because they are responsible for making it work in their classrooms, it is also important to inform and encourage participation from all the other stakeholders in this enterprise–the students, the administrators, the parents, and the community.

Chapter Review: The Tired Teacher's Book Report

Write a 200-word essay, giving your own frank, honest, independent, unbiased, unencumbered opinion as to why you found this chapter to be the most wonderful chapter in the whole world.

Or perhaps not . . .

Chapter 4

Getting Strategized

Planning the Assessment Strategies and Choosing the Assessment Tools

In This Chapter

Now It's Time to Choose Our Assessment Strategies and Our Assessment Tools

To recap: In the past, we tended to rely on only one kind of instrument–the test–to do all of our assessment work for us. We became so wedded to this instrument that much of our thinking about assessment is still subtly influenced by testing. Attempts to break away from the test were often seen as substitutes or alternatives to testing. For example, teachers sought to replace testing with "kid-watching" and observational approaches. Currently, for many teachers, the portfolio has become the one and only "assessment instrument of choice."

The system of assessment being described in this book takes a different approach. We want to encourage teachers to employ a range of assessment strategies–not just one–and develop a repertoire of assessment techniques, or tools, to apply these strategies. The aim is to empower teachers to choose the best combination of approaches for the particular learning they are attempting to evaluate.

We also want teachers to try to make the assessment an organic part of their instruction and recognize that many of the things we do in the name of instruction are, in fact, assessment approaches, too. We believe this will mean less work for teachers and more time for instruction. We also believe it will mean more effective instruction and learning, and the assessment information we share with students and parents will be more helpful and meaningful.

As for the survey-type information administrators need for accountability purposes, we will show how this, too, can be easily derived from the assessment information the teacher gathers primarily for instructional purposes. In other words, as an assessment system, it is a "one-stop shop," offering a range of "merchandise" for all occasions!

Six Key Assessment Strategies

There are six main ways we can go about gathering information on our students' learning growth:

1. We can observe the learners while they are learning. That's right–we just look at them and see what they're doing!
2. We can interact with the learners as they are learning. We can ask questions, prompt, probe, model, introduce expectations, encourage,

critique, give feedback, scaffold the learning to see what happens, modify the task to see how well they manage, and lead our students on to new tasks–all the while praising and applauding, coaxing and directing.

3. We can help the learner "re-create" the learning. This might involve retelling what happened, or changing the viewpoint by taking on a role, or changing the mode of expression–for example, by turning a verbal idea into a visual idea, or by using drama to explore the consequences and implications of a story the students have read.
4. We can reflect on the learning and encourage the learners to reflect, too.
5. We can simulate the learning behavior "artificially" with a test or similar instrument.
6. We can collect learning artifacts or products of learning to document or authenticate our assessment of the learning.

But We Also Need Techniques and Tools to Help Us Secure and Record Assessment Data

Of course, much of our assessment and evaluation will be incidental and will have no other overt form except that it underscores all the choices we make as teachers every moment of the teaching day–such as our choice to stretch a discussion or bring an activity to a conclusion, to intervene in the learning or hold off and wait to see how far the learners can go on their own, to probe with a question, to critique and redirect, to facilitate discovery and applaud achievement–in fact, just about all the things we do to facilitate learning.

But we cannot remember everything we observe. Nor can we, in the heat of a learning episode, grasp the significance of every learning behavior or watch every child with equal vigilance and concentration. As part of our evaluation and planning, we need to be able to reflect on the learning, and for this we need data. This means we need tools and techniques that enable us to secure and record accurate and useful data on the children's learning in a systematic and professionally sound way.

Fortunately, there are no shortages of assessment tools available–there are enough, in fact, to fill a veritable Assessment Toolbox!

A Big Welcome for the Learning Assessment Toolbox, Please!

The toolbox is summarized below. It is formatted like a computer screen. Across the top are the strategy "buttons," and below each button is a "pull-down menu" offering a range of tool options for achieving the strategy heading.

The Learning Assessment Toolbox

Strategies → (column headings); Tools → (entries below)

Observation	Interaction	Re-creation	Reflection	Simulation	Artifact Collection
Anecdotal notebook Page 55	Questioning Page 65	Moving the learning around the language bases Page 74	Self-portraits Page 82	Standardized tests Page 95	Learner-managed learning portfolios Page 100
Anecdotal record card system Page 56	Chat Checks Page 67	Retelling Page 76	Peer portraits Page 83	Teacher-made tests Page 96	Teacher-managed learning portfolios Page 102
Anecedotal computer file Page 56	Conferences Page 69	Rewrites Page 76	Teacher's confidential file Page 83	Testing in pairs Page 98	Video portfolios Page 103
Post-it mail label learning log Page 57	Our class experts Page 71	Picture retellings Page 77	All about me Page 85	Socio-graphs Page 99	Reading logs Page 103
Class log Page 57	Talking stick Page 72	Dramatization Page 78	My computer dossier Page 86	Self-testing Chapter 5	Mini time capsules Page 104
Discussions log Page 58	Fish bowl Page 74	Role-play Page 79	Student autobiographies Page 87		Friday folders Chapter 5
Camera in the classroom Page 59	Dear Author Chapter 5	In-role interviews Page 79	Who am I? Partner interviews Page 87		The "Great home Bulletin Board Competition" Chapter 5
Audio reading record Page 60	Today's heroes Chapter 5	Freeze frame Page 80	Personal journals Page 88		
Video learning log Page 61		Action replay Page 80	Goal setting Page 89		
Think alouds Page 62		Tableaux Page 81	Students' "Things I know and can do" log Page 90		
Running Records Page 63		What did you do at school today? Chapter 5	My art dossier Page 91		
Continuums Page 65			Things I want to write about Page 92		
			Personal video log Page 93		
			"How I Feel About" checklists" Page 94		
			My Eurekas! Page 94		
			Star of the week Chapter 5		
			My future challenges Chapter 5		
			The learning detective Chapter 5		
			Viewpoints Chapter 5		

Using the Learning Assessment Toolbox: An Overview

Later in this chapter, we will examine the strategies and tools listed in the assessment toolbox in more detail. In particular, we'll look at various ways of using them in the classroom. But before we get lost in the details, it's important to get a general idea as to how this all works–a Toolbox Overview, if you will.

The story so far...

Let's review our assessment steps. First, we thought about what assessment is, and in the process of refining our conception of assessment, we rejected a range of misconceptions. Then we thought about the *Who* question: Who are we doing the assessment for? To answer this question, we did an assessment audit, which helped us focus on our learning and, thus, our assessment stakeholders. Then we asked the *What* question: What are we going to be assessing? The answer, of course, was learning. But before we could plan our assessment approaches, we needed to plan the learning. So we did that. We prepared a Learning Assessment Plan, which set out the learning we hoped to facilitate.

Now we're going to think about how we are going to assess the learning. We'll think about the strategies we will use and the tools and techniques we might find useful to help us apply those strategies. That's right–we're about to complete the next two columns in the Learning Assessment Plan!

Learning Assessment Plan for the following Grade Range:_____ to _____

Subjects (Learning Areas)	Learning Outcomes	Assessment Strategies	Assessment Tools
	READING (continued)		
	Skills and Strategies *(Able to . . .)*		
	Use an index to locate information in the text		
	Attitudes and Values *(Feels and believes about self and learning . . .)*		

In order to do this, the teacher takes each learning outcome and uses the strategies and the tools from the toolbox as planning prompts.

But first a few introductory points:

- The whole purpose of the toolbox is to prompt us with ideas as we plan our assessment approaches.

- The tools themselves are categorized according to the main assessment strategies they support–but, of course, many of these techniques and ideas could be used to support a number of assessment strategies.

- Furthermore, many of the suggestions described here are as much teaching ideas as assessment ideas–and, in view of the things we've been saying in earlier chapters, this shouldn't come as a great surprise. One of the main aims of this book is to show how assessment and learning need to be organically interrelated and mutually supportive.

- We hope that teachers will feel free to use these ideas. But better still, we hope they feel empowered to construct their own ways of applying the strategies to their instruction–to find new and effective ways to observe student learning and find out more about it (by interacting with it, re-creating it, reflecting on it, or simulating it), and to document and therefore facilitate both learning and assessment by keeping and studying learning artifacts.

So now, let's walk through, or better still, "think aloud," our way through this process. If the learning outcome was "Able to use an index to locate information," the teacher's thought processes might go something like the scenario on the next page.

Hmmmm. So, I want to know if a student is able to "use an index to locate information." Now, what strategies can I use?

What about ***Observation****? Maybe if I keep an eye on my students when they're reading nonfiction texts, I'll see whether or not they're able to use an index. And I've already decided that I'll keep an anecdotal notebook, so if I do see a child using an index appropriately, I'll make a note in my anecdotal notebook.*

But I guess I should check out the other strategies, too. What about ***Interaction****? Yes, I guess I could ask the students a question about a text and see if they know and are able to use the index to locate the answer. I'll put that down as "questioning."*

What about ***Re-creation****? Maybe if I discover that some of my students have found information in a text, I'll ask them how they found it and get them to retell, or go over the steps they went through, in using the index to find it. That will give me a clear idea as to what they did and what they know about using an index. Or maybe I could ask them to show the steps they went through as a flow diagram?*

Reflection*? Well, when I have a reading conference with a student, if I don't have any other information on this piece of learning–in other words, if Observation, Interaction, and Re-creation don't tell me, I can always ask the children to reflect on their learning and then tell me if they can use an index. I'll put it on my plan, just in case I need to do this to check on this learning outcome. I'm also going to have my students keep their own "I can do" lists, and when they reflect on their own learning, they could enter this skill there, too.*

Simulation*? I guess I could always make up some kind of "test" in which the students have to look up a whole range of information using an index–but that's rather artificial. It makes more sense to make "real" use of an index rather than contrive a situation. So I won't bother with Simulation for this learning outcome.*

Artifact Collection*? I'll be encouraging the students to include an index when they write their own nonfiction books, so maybe I could include any samples of this in their portfolio of work I'm going to keep. They might do this in their own personal student portfolios, too. In fact, I think I'll encourage them to include an index to their own student portfolios! Now, that's a good idea!*

As a result, the notes for this learning outcome would end up looking something like this:

Subjects (Learning Areas)	Learning Outcomes	Assessment Strategies	Assessment Tools
Language Arts			
Reading	Skills and Strategies *(Able to . . .)*		
	Use an index to locate information in the text	***Observation*** ***Interaction*** ***Reflection*** ***Artifact Collection***	***Anecdotal notebook*** ***Questioning (ask the child to find information in a text)*** ***Teacher/Student conference*** ***Student's "I can do" checklist*** ***Teacher portfolio work samples*** ***Student portfolio samples, also index to own portfolio***

Assessment Toolbox Workshop

In the remaining pages of this chapter, we will be giving a brief introduction to most of the tools listed in the toolbox (a few are also found in Chapter 5). They are grouped according to the main assessment strategy they use: observation, interaction, re-creation, reflection, simulation, or artifact collection. But, of course, many of the tools can contribute to more than one assessment strategy.

Assessment Tools That Facilitate Observation

Anecdotal notebook

Main assessment strategy: Observation
Other strategies: Interaction and Reflection

You will need: A notebook, preferably with a cut-away "index" running down the edges of the pages.

This is a notebook in which the teacher records anecdotal observations about the learning. Keep the notebook handy when conducting roving or student conferences so that quick entries can be made when something significant is observed. Each entry should start with the date (so we can observe learning over time). The entries should be brief comments on the learning in terms of:

- what the child: knows/ can do/ feels and believes, or
- is starting to know/ do/ feel and believe, or
- needs to know/ be able to do/ feel and believe.

It's a good idea to share what you are writing in your anecdotal notebook with your students. This sharing can provide motivation ("The teacher is writing something about my work!") and feedback (the students get to know what the teacher thinks about their learning). It also helps students to develop their own assessment skills. When they see how their teacher goes about valuing their work, they can internalize that valuing process and learn to do it for themselves and their peers.

Anecdotal record card system

Main assessment strategy:	Observation
Other strategies:	Interaction and Reflection
You will need:	A set of record cards, one per child, perhaps filed in a ring binder.

This device is similar to the notebook, but in this case, the information is stored on cards, one per student.

Anecdotal computer file

Main assessment strategy:	Observation
Other strategies:	Interaction and Reflection
You will need:	Computer and word processing program

This is similar to the anecdotal notebook or card system, but in this case, the observations are recorded on a computer file.

Post-it, or mail label, learning log

Main assessment strategy:	Observation
Other strategies:	Interaction and Reflection
You will need:	Post-it notes or mail labels and an anecdotal notebook or card system

This device makes use of an anecdotal notebook or card system, but instead of writing the anecdotal observation in the notebook or on a card, the teacher writes it on a post-it or mail label. This is then peeled off and attached to the notebook or record card. One advantage of this system is that when moving around the classroom, the teacher only needs to carry a pack of post-its or mail labels, not a bulky notebook or file.

Another useful variation with upper grades is to leave the post-its with the students and give them the responsibility of pasting them into the teacher's notebook or record card system. One advantage of this approach is that the students are also able to participate in the review of their work and can internalize and learn from the feedback provided. If the comments are primarily positive and helpful, this can be very motivational.

This method can be taken one step further, by encouraging the students to complete their own post-it comments and attach these to their file, too. To help distinguish between teacher and student comments, you might wish to use different colored labels.

Class log

Main assessment strategy:	Observation
Other strategies:	Reflection and Interaction

When children come home from school, the question they are most likely to be asked is, "What happened at school today?" Unfortunately, the response parents hear most often is, "Oh . . . nothing."

I first began keeping a class log with my students to combat this "Oh...nothing Syndrome." But soon it became obvious that it was serving a number of other valuable purposes. This is how I operated it then–but teachers can adapt the procedures to meet their own requirements.

I would introduce the class log as a special activity to keep parents informed and up-to-date with what was happening in the classroom. I would then choose someone to be a class log writer for the day. I made sure the children knew that the log writer was a very special person. For one thing, the writer didn't have to do any other schoolwork. Instead, that special person was to sit in the classroom and be a good reporter, listening and watching everything that was going on. The log writer's job was to write down every important thing that happened in the classroom throughout the day. When we shared our news in the morning, the log writer would make a note of which students shared news and what their items were about. When we wrote our regular shared story together, the log writer would note what it was about. In shared reading, the log writer would note the book we shared.

This went on until five minutes before the end of the day. I would make sure the class had everything completely cleaned up before this, and then we would all sit and listen while the log writer read aloud what had happened and who had "made the news." It proved to be an excellent way to review the day, and when they went home, the children had already had their memories primed so they were able to tell their parents everything, and often in minute detail! The next day, a new log writer took over the task. As for the writer not having to do any other schoolwork–that was a little bit of a confidence trick, because children don't like to be all that different from their peers. As a result, usually the student not only wrote the class log but also did most, if not all, of the schoolwork!

The big spin-off for me was that the log also proved a superb assessment device. It reflected the day's learning to me, but through the eyes of a student. It frequently made me rethink what had happened during the day, especially when I had to reconcile what I thought had happened with what the log writer had observed and written about.

One further point, in SSR (Sustained Silent Reading) time, the class log was almost always the most popular book in the entire class library!

Discussion logs

Main assessment strategy:	Observation
Other strategies:	Reflection and Interaction
You will need:	A score sheet and clipboard along with a watch that indicates the seconds.

This is a simple and engaging device than can sometimes tell us a great deal about who does all the talking in the classroom–and who doesn't! One student with a watch that shows the seconds is given a clipboard with everyone's name on it–the teacher's as well as the students'. The class then conducts a discussion on some topic or instructional material. The student with the clipboard keeps an eye on the watch, and every fifteen seconds, looks to see who is talking. A check mark is put next to the person's name. If more than one person is talking, a check mark is placed next to both or all of their names!

At the end of the discussion period, or an agreed upon period of time, tally up the number of checks for each person. Discuss the data with the class. If some people seem to have had more to say than others, talk about ways of sharing the time and discussion more equitably. Likewise, if some people have not had a chance to say anything, talk about things the group can do to help everyone have their say.

This device can be valuable for the teacher because it gives some indication as to the students' oral language confidence, their awareness and sensitivity to each other, and the extent to which the teacher or particular students dominate the group.

When you're finished, your Discussion Log might look something like this:

Discussion Log: Grade 3	
Teacher	√ √ √ √ √ √ √ √ √ √
Moira	√
Adam	√ √ √ √ √ √ √ √ √
Noona	√ √ √ √
Zak	√
Quentin	
Zelda	√ √ √ √ √ √
Tina	√
Pablo	
Blake	√ √ √
Arlo	√
Tracy	

Camera in the classroom

Main assessment strategy: Observation
Other strategies: Interaction, Reflection, Artifact Collection
You will need: A camera

A camera in the classroom is a wonderful observational tool. Keep it handy and snap pictures of the children in significant learning situations. It doesn't have to be an extraordinary camera –a cheap, disposable type is a great option.

When the photos are printed, display them with the students' work–that way, process and product are presented together. A regular class photo bulletin board is a good idea, too–it can be a reminder of, and a pleasant way of reviewing, previous class projects. The possibility that the students might be featured in the next batch of photos can also be a good motivator.

A group of students might like to use the photographs to prepare a class "big book" to show how a topic was studied or to "log" some aspects of the class program. The teacher might then let the students take this home in turns to share with their parents. These examples of "classroom photojournalism" are often very popular during Sustained Silent Reading sessions.

In addition to "observing" the learning, other assessment strategies might be served by the use of a camera. For example, class photographic logs can be used to help students *reflect* on their learning, and the photos are excellent for *learning artifact* collection.

As for the expense of having the photos processed, you might try what one resourceful teacher did–she approached her local photo processing firm and talked them into letting her have the disposable cameras for free, provided she put a notice acknowledging the firm's support alongside the class photo wall! (Advertising in the classroom? That's an ethical matter you can judge for yourself!)

Audio reading record

Main assessment strategy:	Observation
Other strategies:	Interaction, Reflection, Artifact Collection
You will need:	A tape recorder, and a cassette for each child

When working with emergent and early readers, it is often useful to keep a cassette tape for each child and regularly–say once a month–record the students as they read a short extract from a text they are currently covering. Before each excerpt, record the date and the name of the text the child is going to read from. Choose texts the student is familiar with, so that the reading is a positive experience.

Listening to the tape might provide some insight into the child's reading strategies, attitude toward reading, and level of confidence. When the recording is completed, it's a good idea to play the tape back and listen to it with the child. While you're both listening to it, encourage the child to talk about the story. Talk about the reading strategies the child is using, too.

Sometimes you can gain interesting insights into the student's reading strategy repertoire. It also helps to be able to verbalize about strategies.

"You weren't sure what that word was, were you? But you did a clever thing. Did you notice what you did?"

"That was interesting. What were you doing there?"

"Tell me how you worked that out."

"Why do you think the character did that?"

In addition to making use of observation, the audio reading tape also enables us to use a number of other strategies. In particular, we can use interaction and reflection when we listen to the taped reading and talk about it with the student. Then we use artifact collection when we add the tape to the student's portfolio.

Video learning log

Main assessment strategy:	Observation
Other strategies:	Reflection and Artifact Collection
You will need:	A videocamera and videotapes

The videocamera not only helps us "observe"–after all, you have to look through the viewfinder and choose, focus, and frame your shots–but you are also able to look at the videotapes afterward and reflect on the learning.

There are a number of ways you can use the videocamera. The simplest is to have the camera available at all times and tape anything that seems to be significant or memorable. The main drawback with this very open-ended approach is that you end up with hours of nebulous, and often somewhat boring, footage–the equivalent of your best friend's tiresome holiday slide show! In short, it pays to plan what you intend to videotape and be selective about it. The following are some useful ways to do this.

Subject video logs

Keep one tape for each subject area, and systematically film the children working in that area throughout the term or the year. Use the video for your own reflection, to record and document progress, and to share with and inform the parents.

Event videos

Keep a video for particular events or major learning experiences, such as a trip, classroom visitor, or class production. Use the video for reviewing the experience with your students.

Student mini-documentaries

This provides an opportunity for everyone to have fifteen minutes of fame! You will need a videotape for each student in your class. Tell the children that you want to make a fifteen-minute video of everyone in the classroom, showing what they are working on this year, what their achievements are, and what they would like others to know about them. Each student then has to plan his or her own mini-documentary, with suggestions for video location, the nature of the shots, a storyboard to assist production, a time frame for each segment, and scripted material for introduction, links, and conclusion. Older students might be able to prepare and do much of the production themselves. The fifteen-minute time frame is vital because it will compel the students to be selective and disciplined about the task. It also ensures that sharing of the mini-documentaries doesn't turn into a marathon of video-watching! The finished mini-documentary can be taken home to share with the student's family and then filed in the student's portfolio.

Time-lapse video documentary

The teacher who first tried this idea came up with it after seeing a similar method depicted in a film. In the movie, a character had taken a still photo of the same scene at the same time on a particular day of the week over a period of years. So the teacher set up the videocamera on a tripod in her classroom and left it taping for exactly two minutes, from 9:30 to 9:32, every Thursday morning for an entire term. The camera was set up in the same location each time and set to film the same wide-angle shot of the classroom. Each taping was prefaced with a graphic indicating the day, date, and time. At the end of the term, the students watched the video and had an engrossing discussion on what had changed during the term and what had stayed the same. They looked at the wall displays, the class activities, their clothes, the weather, even what the teacher was doing and wearing!

Think alouds

Main assessment strategy: Observation
Other strategies: Interaction and Reflection

Teachers introduce the students to "Think alouds" by modeling them in a class activity. For example, for Shared Writing, the teachers might compose a story on a large sheet of paper or an overhead transparency, with the students watching and "listening in." The teachers not only write but also talk aloud the thoughts going through their head as they write. If this is the first time the teachers have used the "think aloud" process, they might want to introduce the process to the students, too. Their commentary might go like this:

"Today I'm going to 'think aloud' my way through a story I want to write. I'm actually going to let you hear what is going on inside my head. I have my page ready for my first draft. And I know what I want to write about because I've been thinking about it ever since it happened. It's about what happened after school yesterday. I'd better make sure my readers know when and where this story is taking place, so I think that's how I'll start.

Yesterday, after school, when all the children had gone home, I was sitting at my desk, pondering what I was going to have for dinner.... No, I don't like 'pondering.' It sounds too ... heavy. I think I'll go for something simple... like 'thinking about'... sitting at my desk, thinking about what I was going to have for dinner, when suddenly..."

The students can be encouraged to "think aloud" in any subject of the curriculum, but this technique is particularly useful in language arts, mathematics, and science.

The value to the teacher is that it provides an insight into the mental processes the child is using, which, of course, is vital for assessment. But it is useful for the students as well, because they learn to verbalize their understanding of the process.

Students can also do this in pairs–one working and "thinking aloud," and the other listening and interacting.

Running records

Main assessment strategy: Observation
Additional strategy: Reflection

The taking of "running records" was developed by Marie Clay for the close monitoring of the learning being done by emergent readers. In essence, it is a very simple and transparently authentic assessment device. What better way to check on reading progress than to observe what the student does while reading? The taking of "running records" for emergent readers is fully discussed by Clay in her book, *The Early Detection of Reading Difficulties (3rd Edition)* (Heinemann, 1985), beginning on Page 17. There is also helpful material in *Reading in Junior Classes* (Learning Media, Ministry of Education, Wellington) and *ERIC, Early Reading In-service Course,* Units 2 and 3, available on the Internet, and in *Knowing Literacy: Constructive Literacy Assessment,* by Peter Johnston (Stenhouse, York, Maine, 1997).

Briefly, the teacher listens and observes while the child reads from a text. This can be a familiar story (the most recent book the child has completed) or an unfamiliar story. A familiar story is used if the teacher wants to check to see if the difficulty level of the reading material is appropriate for the child, and to see how well the child is able to use the reading strategies that have been taught. An unfamiliar text is used if the teacher wants to see if the child has the confidence to take risks and is able to independently integrate the strategies that have been taught.

While the child reads, the teacher listens, observes, and takes notes. Publishers have provided special "running record" forms, and many teachers use these. However, once teachers are proficient with running records, it is just as easy to put checks on an ordinary piece of paper, changing the line for each new line of text. Some teachers prefer to tape record the running record and analyze it after the reading. These tapes can be kept as documentation of the learning, too (see Audio Reading Record, Page 60).

The teacher puts a check mark for each word correctly read and notes any miscues or other significant behavior, such as self-corrections, repeats, omissions, starting over again, etc. The teacher also notes the strategies being used by the child. The teacher doesn't intervene in the reading unless the child comes to a halt. When the student has finished reading, the teacher might want to check on the depth of understanding by asking a few questions about the text or asking the child to retell the story.

In addition to the information gained by observing what the child actually does while reading, the miscue data can be numerically analyzed. An "error rate" can be established by dividing the number of errors by the number of words in the text and multiplying the answer by 100 to give us an error rate as a percentage. For example, if a child makes 5 errors in a text with 125 words, the error rate would be calculated as follows:

$$\frac{5 \times 100}{125} = 4$$

The value of running records is that they not only give valuable information on reading strategies and competence but also, when regular records are kept, the teacher is able to make comparisons with previous data to show progress over time.

Wider use of the concept of "running records"

The notion of taking regular "soundings" of a child's learning in this way is a valuable one that has applications in areas other than reading. Taking regular writing samples enables the teacher to develop a similar appreciation of a child's learning progress over time. The samples can be evaluated by checking them against the specific learning outcomes for written language in the Learning Assessment Record.

It is also possible to apply the concept of running records to mathematics, physical education, and in a somewhat looser fashion, with regular interviews, in science, and social studies.

Continuums

Main assessment strategy: Observation
Additional strategy: Reflection

Much significant learning develops in an evolutionary way. The teacher who focuses on separate elements of learning is in danger of losing a sense of the holistic and interrelated nature of much learning. When learning to write, for example, there are many important elements in the act of writing.

Sometimes it is helpful to group a number of characteristics together which, when most are in evidence, indicate a significant "level" of maturity. There have been a number of attempts to provide such developmental rubrics.

Assessment Tools That Facilitate Interaction

Questioning

Main assessment strategy: Interaction
Other strategies: Observation and Reflection

We all know about questioning–it's an essential instructional tool. But it is helpful to remember that there are different kinds of questions, and each type of question might serve a different instructional purpose.

- Closed questions are ones in which there is a single correct response. Teachers are sometimes criticized for relying too heavily on this kind of interaction because it tends to convey the notion that all questions and problems have a single right answer. In that respect, closed questions curtail further thought or creative ideas. In fact, many very difficult problems might have a whole range of answers, and some of these might be more applicable than others in certain situations. Closed questions also might encourage a reliance on "binary thinking." (See misconception number 6 on Page 14.) Multiple-choice tests have been criticized for straight-jacketing thinking in this way, too.

- Open-ended questions are ones that invite a more sustained response. They are useful in situations where we want our students to follow a line of thought, develop a number of ideas, pursue relationships between a number of things, or sustain an argument.

- Probe questions are good for "pushing" your students' thinking.

Just as there are different kinds of questions, there are also a number of ways in which teachers can respond to students' answers.

- We can legislate–say its right or wrong.

- We can correct–provide a right answer.

- We can rephrase the question.

- We can redirect the question.

- We can acknowledge the response without passing judgment, usually with a nod of the head or responses like, "Uh huh!" "Hmmm," or, "I can hear what you're saying."

- And we can do all the above with varying degrees of emotional connotation ranging from elation to anger and hostility to support.

Just as it's valuable to vary the kinds of questions we ask, it's also helpful to vary the kinds of responses we give to the students' answers. The important thing is to do what best serves the instructional purpose and meets the learners' needs.

Obviously we will not want or need or even be able to record all responses to incidental classroom questioning! But there are some responses that give valuable or significant insight into student learning, or that suggest something we should subsequently deal with or build on. For such situations, it helps to have some kind of anecdotal recording system operating in your classroom.

Chat checks

Main assessment strategy:	Interaction
Additional strategy:	Reflection
You will need:	Chat Check form for the class and some kind of anecdotal notebook or record card system

Conversation is a wonderful, nonthreatening assessment device! When we chat informally, we can gain significant insight into what students know or can do–especially their feelings or attitudes toward the learning program, toward themselves, and toward the teacher and the class. Keep notes of significant insights in an anecdotal notebook, file, or record card.

These conversations also provide opportunities to interact with your students and positively explore their attitudes and values. A casual conversation with the teacher can sometimes provide a much-needed "buzz" for a student. It can revive student enthusiasm and commitment as well as provide opportunities for the student to seek support and reassurance. What you talk about might not be very important. Its significance is often symbolic, because it is interpreted by the student as recognition or validation . "*She chose to talk to me! She acknowledged that I exist! She cares about what I do and think.*"

However, not all children will seek out an opportunity for a chat with the teacher. Some children are shy or insecure, or naturally introverted and self-sufficient. It is also very easy in a busy classroom to overlook some children–usually the industrious, non-troublesome students! One way to make sure we are not leaving anyone out is to keep a Chat Check. Use a class roll and at the end of each week, sit down with the list and put a check mark beside the names of students with whom you can recall having some form of interactive chat during the week.

When you're finished, your Chat Check might look something like the chart on the next page.

My Chat Check

Names	9/7	9/14	9/21	9/28	10/5	10/12	10/19	10/26	11/2	11/9
Moira	√√	√√		√	√					
Adam	√		√√		√					
Noona	√		√√	√	√					
Zak	√				√√					
Quentin			√							
Zelda		√			√					
Tina			√	√√						
Pablo	√					√				
Blake			√	√	√					
Arlo		√								
Tracy			√√	√	√					

Conferences

Main assessment strategy: Interaction
Other strategies: Reflection and Observation
You will need: An anecdotal recording system

A conference is basically people talking together with a purpose. They are "conferring." This, of course, is an obvious and commonplace part of instruction, but we include it here to remind ourselves that it is also an excellent opportunity to check on the learning–to critique it, extend it, redirect it, refocus it, and scaffold it in preparation for the next learning challenge. This is our chance to give helpful feedback, and to applaud the learning and help build positive and empowering attitudes.

One tends to think of conferencing as something the teacher does for or to the student, but it is important to encourage students to initiate conferences, too. Conferences also provide opportunities for student self-assessment and peer assessment as well as teacher assessment.

Conferences can involve any number of people. They might be:

Individual conferences, in which the teacher works one-on-one with the student, or the student seeks one-on-one help from the teacher.

Roving conferences, when the teacher makes short calls on each child to find out "how it's going." In these situations, it is important to gauge three pieces of information before intervening in the task:

- the context (What is the child actually doing?);
- the location within the context (What part of the task is the child dealing with at the moment?);
- the perceived challenges, problems, or difficulties (What does the child think he or she needs help with at the moment?).

Partner conferences, in which students get together in pairs (the "buddy system").

Group conferences, in which groups of students get together to confer–with or without the teacher. It is helpful to give a group some kind of structure to assist them with evaluative tasks.

Another approach is to provide a detailed group evaluation form like the one on the next page.

“How Are We Doing?”

Our Group Conference Report

1. What have you been working on? Make up a “title” or a short sentence that sums up what you’ve been doing.

2. What did you actually do? (Just write headings, or, if you prefer, draw a diagram.)

3. What were some of the best things you did?

4. What are some of the things you need more help with or found difficult?

5. What do you think you should do next ? (What are you going to work on or try to do now?)

Our class experts

Main assessment strategy:	Interaction
Other strategies:	Reflection and Observation
You will need:	A display board or bulletin board headed "Our Class Experts"

Using this technique, the teacher explains to the students that we all have our own special areas of knowledge and expertise–some children might be good at tying knots; some might know a lot about bicycles; some might have pets and know how to look after them; some might be good at using a dictionary or a thesaurus; some might know how to do useful things on the computer; some might know how to speak several languages; some might have interesting collections or have traveled to unusual places. The teacher encourages the students to think of something for which they can be the class expert. When they have thought of something, they enter it alongside their name on the "Our Class Experts" list. That lets the other students know that if they need to know more about that particular topic, they can come to "the expert."

The list doesn't have to be completed quickly –it's a good idea to let the students have time to think about their area of expertise. Sometimes the teacher can help by prompting: *"Jennifer, you seem to know when to use apostrophes. I think you should be our class expert on apostrophes."*

Keep in mind, the students can be class experts on more than one topic. They can also set out to make themselves experts on a particular subject. For example, one student might decide to be an expert on dinosaurs, so he or she researches the topic and finds out as much as possible. As a "class expert," that student has a responsibility to share his or her interest and knowledge with the other students. This means keeping up-to-date on the chosen topic, looking for news items that relate to the topic, finding books on the topic to display in the class library, giving talks on the topic, answering questions when they arise, and writing articles and books on the subject for the other students to read. Students can help each other by passing relevant information on to the appropriate class expert. The information might be in the form of newspaper and magazine clippings or books they have read that relate to that person's area of expertise.

As an assessment tool, the "Class Experts" list gives teachers valuable information on student interests and attitudes. It can help us really get to know our students, and it's useful when we're suggesting topics for personal writing and research.

Your "Class Experts" list might look something like this:

Our Class Experts!

Names	**Ask me about ...**
Moira	Marsupials, Multiplication tables
Adam	Disneyland, Ants, Introducing a speaker to the class
Noona	Apostrophes, Making paper
Zak	Frogs
Quentin	Knights and castles, Canons
Zelda	Whales, Other sea mammals
Tina	Fossils, Rocks
Pablo	Magic tricks
Blake	
Arlo	Making pizza, Collecting stamps
Tracy	Kite flying

Talking stick

Main assessment strategy: Interaction
Other strategies: Reflection and Observation
You will need: Something to use initially as a "talking stick." This could be an interesting piece of wood or one that someone has actually colored or carved. As an alternative, you could use a symbolic talking stick–a pen or a ruler.

The talking stick is an excellent way to give everyone in the classroom an opportunity to speak up and be heard. Everyone, including the teacher, sits in a circle facing one another. The teacher explains that in some parts of the ancient world, people solved their problems by talking about them and sharing them. The introduction goes something like the quote on the next page.

"They decided that the first secret to solving problems is to give everybody an opportunity to speak. They did this by gathering in 'talking circles' like this one. The next secret was to make sure everyone listened and didn't interrupt. They did this by using a special carved stick, which they called the 'talking stick.' The talking stick was passed around the circle from person to person. Only the person holding the talking stick was allowed to speak. The others were not allowed to interrupt, interject, or even comment. The only thing anyone else was allowed to say was 'thank you' when the person had finished speaking. When one person had finished speaking, the talking stick was passed to the next person in the circle. But if that person didn't want to say anything, he or she could say 'thank you' and pass the stick to the next person. Once the stick had come back to where it started, it was placed on the ground in the center of the circle. That meant that the 'round' was over. Then, anyone who wanted to could talk or comment or disagree."

Then the teacher explains that this is what the class is going to do. The "rules" are the same as they were in ancient times.

- The teacher (perhaps with student collaboration) defines the subject for the round or the question for deliberation.
- Only the person with the talking stick can talk; everyone else (including the teacher) listens respectfully.
- Only when the talking stick is placed on the ground in the center of the circle is anyone allowed to interrupt or comment.

It is important to frame the question or topic for discussion clearly so the students know what they are expected to talk about. The following are some examples to get you thinking.

We have just returned from our trip to the heritage park. What was the best part of the trip for you?

Our school playground is very untidy because people are always dropping litter. How do you feel about this, and what do you think we should do about it?

We have now completed our puppet show. What did we learn from doing this project?

I wonder if you can remember what happened and how you felt on your very first day at school? When the talking stick comes to you, if you can remember something and would like to share it with us all, please do.

As the talking stick is making its rounds, the teacher observes the students carefully and listens closely to what they have to say. Later, the teacher makes a note of any significant assessment information.

Fish bowl

Main assessment strategy: Interaction
Other strategies: Reflection and Observation

This is a valuable assessment device for both the teacher and the students. A number of students are chosen to take part in a group activity. It could be a discussion on the topic the class is studying at the moment, or planning something such as a collaborative publication or display.

The group sits in a circle in the middle of the classroom. The rest of the students sit in a bigger circle around the outside. The teacher explains that the students in the middle are the "goldfish in a goldfish bowl." The others are the observers, watching the goldfish! It is often helpful for the teacher to join the goldfish group and help them model the required behavior.

When the discussion or activity is over, the goldfish relax and the observers talk about what they saw happening and what they thought about the discussion points. Listening to the students' responses often provides a clear insight into their understanding of what is being studied and the attitudes and values they hold about the curriculum. The teacher records significant insights in an anecdotal notebook, file, or record card.

Assessment Tools That Facilitate Re-creation

Moving the learning around the language bases

Main assessment strategy: Re-creation
Other strategies: Observation and Interaction

This technique lies behind most of the re-creation activities discussed in this section. The Language Arts are seen as encompassing four different kinds of "languages." These can be summarized as follows:

In **oral language**, we use a system of culturally significant sounds to convey our ideas, and we draw on the modes of talking and listening.

In **written language**, we use a system of significant symbols (letters and punctuation) to present our ideas, and we draw on the modes of reading and writing.

In **visual language**, we use significant images and imagery (pictures, photographs, video, diagrams, maps, charts, and also typography and layout) to convey our ideas, and the modes we use are presenting and viewing.

With **body language**, we use significant movements and gestures (including facial expressions and the interactive use of space, dance, drama, and the like). We convey our ideas by *performing them* and receive them by watching.[1]

For the purposes of this exercise, we imagine the languages as a kind of baseball diamond.

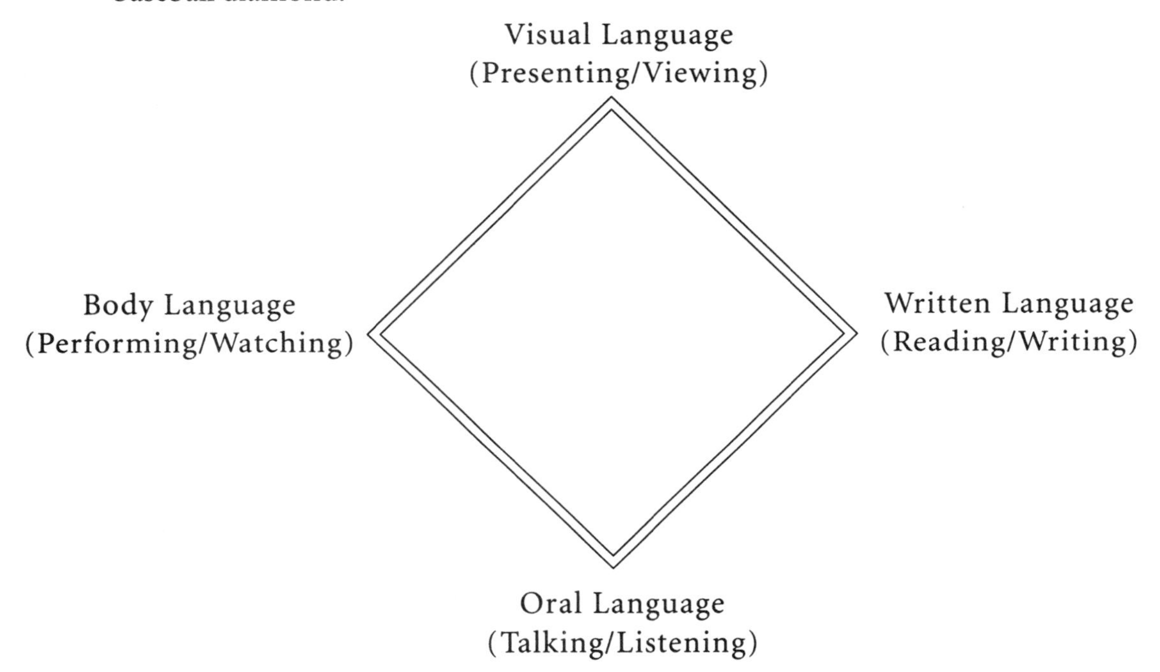

The "game" can start on any base. One student might begin by reading a story. To assess and extend the learning, we might then take that story and move to a different language base–for example, visual language–and turn the story into a visual presentation. This could be in the form of a story board (see Picture Retellings, Page 76). Or you might move to the body language base and dramatize it, or move to the oral language base and tell the story orally (see Retellings, next page).

You can also change the mode on the same base. For example, after reading a story a student might prepare a written version, or an innovation on the text (see Rewrites, next page). Or after hearing a story, a student might retell it in his or her own words. Similarly, after viewing a videotape, the students could prepare their own video version of what they've seen.

---

[1] Inside New Zealand Classrooms, by Alan Trussell-Cullen, Richard C. Owens, Katonah, New York (1996): Page 11.

Some teachers might say, "But this is an instructional technique." And so it is, but then, as we have been emphasizing throughout this text, the ideal situation is for instruction and assessment to be organically interwoven like this.

Retellings

Main assessment strategy: Re-creation
Additional strategy: Interaction

Retellings are an excellent way to gain insight into our students' understanding of concepts or ideas, and their grasp of sequence and process. It is a technique that is often used in emergent reading. The teacher asks the children to retell a story in their own words and then listens in a positive and encouraging way to see to what extent the students have read and understood the text. At the same time, the teacher can gain some insight into the strategies the children might have used to arrive at that understanding.

However, the device can be used with students of any age, and it often is. High school students of literature, for example, might be asked to retell the story line of a novel, play, or movie to show that they have grasped the denouement and the forces of theme and character at work in the text.

Retellings can be used in other subject areas, too. In science, for example, a student might be asked to recount a sequence of events, such as after witnessing a butterfly emerging from its chrysalis, or to describe a process, such as when particular chemicals were brought together or a magnet was placed under a paper on which iron filings were spread. In mathematics, a retelling might involve explaining a process explored with manipulatives. In social studies, it could involve recounting an historical event. In each case, the important question is not, "Did the student remember all the details accurately?" But rather, "Did the student make connections with other experiences or grasp the implications of the detail, or follow and understand the process?"

Rewrites

Main assessment strategy: Re-creation
Other strategies: Interaction and Reflection

Rewrites are sometimes given the grandiose title: "Innovations on a text." After reading a story or nonfiction text, the students are encouraged, either as a shared writing activity or as an independent writing activity, to create a new text using elements of the original. So *I've Been Eating Blackberries*, by Alan

Trussell-Cullen, could become *We've Been Eating Chocolate Cake*, by the first grade students at Jack Jackter Elementary School. Or a book on looking after pet dogs might become a class-authored book on taking care of pet cats.

- The rewrite (or innovation) can focus on the structure of the original story. For example, the story of the *Three Little Pigs* might become the story of the *Three Little Fur Seals.*
- It might focus on recurring language elements. For example, a rewrite of *The Little Red Hen* could make use of the recurring phrases, "*Who will help me,*" and, "*Then I will do it myself!*" *And she did.*
- The rewrite might involve moving the story to a new geographical location. For example, a story set in an African village could be moved to a location in suburban North America.
- It might involve a shift in time. For example, a story about medieval knights might be transferred to the 20th century.

Rewrites are valuable assessment tools because they enable us to see to what extent our students have understood and appreciated the original text. The rewrites might also show us to what extent our students grasp the significance of the way the mimicked author uses language, plot, metaphor, and other literary devices, and the extent to which the students can apply language knowledge and skills acquired from the study of reading in their own writing.

Picture retellings

Main assessment strategy: Re-creation
Additional strategy: Interaction

A picture retelling is similar to a rewrite, but instead of moving story elements to a new story, students are encouraged to visually represent the story or some of its key elements.

In making this transfer from the verbal to the visual realm, students can show how well they understood and appreciated the original text. Talking about the students' visual creations with them in a positive and respectful way could yield even more significant insights into their response to the original text.

Significant assessment data can be recorded in some form of anecdotal notebook, file, or record card. Some of the artwork could also go into the student's or the teacher's portfolio.

Dramatization

Main assessment strategy:	Re-creation
Other strategies:	Interaction and Observation

As we discussed under "Moving the Learning Around the Language Bases," an effective way to both extend and assess student learning is to change the mode in which the students have experienced the learning. For example, if your students have read and written about a particular topic or event, you can gain further insight into their learning by having them re-create elements of the learning in dramatic form.

This device is particularly useful in literary and historical studies where the students retell a story or re-create an historical event. However, by using a little imagination, it is possible to dramatize scientific learning, too. For example, the students might dramatize environmental issues, or depict in stylized form the movement of the planets in our solar system or even molecular equations.

Our mind-set tends to require a written "script" as a starting point for dramatization. Yet so often the need to have everything written down first restricts students' dramatic imagination. Besides, drama is often conveyed more by what we *don't* say than by what we *do* say, and by our gestures, movements, and groupings, and the way we interpret and use space. Furthermore, the script tends to "fix" the performance and restrict the scope for improvisation and innovation. It is often better to begin to create the dramatic action through experimentation and collaboration and to subsequently generate the script.

For assessment purposes, this is a more useful way to proceed because it enables us to observe and interact with our students as they discuss and refine their ideas and interpretations. By doing so, we can gain many valuable insights into what they have understood from the learning, how they are able to apply what they have learned, and how the learning has affected their attitudes and values. Significant assessment data can be recorded in some form of anecdotal notebook, file, or record card.

Technical additions such as lighting, makeup, costuming, set design, sound effects, and music can also contribute to the meaning; but too much attention to these things tends to distract from what the performance is trying to convey.

Role-play

Main assessment strategy: Re-creation
Additional strategy: Interaction

Taking on a character role is often an excellent way to assist students in exploring attitudes and ideas about values. A simple prop, such as a hat, a pair of glasses, or a piece of material draped across the shoulders, can quickly establish character. Simple "agit-prop" devices such as signs and labels are often helpful for establishing where we are in time and location. For example, *AT HOME*, or *LATER THAT DAY*. Composite roles (a number of people acting as one person) are fun to use, too.

In-role interviews

Main assessment strategy: Re-creation
Additional strategy: Interaction

For this activity, the students are encouraged to take on a role related to the subject they have been studying. They are then interviewed in that role. The teacher listens, observes, and notes any significant revelations as to what the students know about the topic under study, the skills they are able to use, and the attitudes and values they demonstrate.

This activity works well in a range of subject contexts, from language and literature studies to the social sciences and civics. For example, as part of an historical and language arts study, the students might have been reading about the origins of the nursery rhyme "Jack be nimble, Jack be quick," in *A Pocketful of Posies*. The teacher might decide to explore the students' understanding and appreciation of the life and plight of 18th century lacemakers by having them research the subject and then act out this role. The teacher would then interview the lacemakers and ask them why they sang this song and how they felt as they played the rather sad and desperate game that lacemakers used to play while reciting this nursery rhyme.

In-role interviews are particularly useful for exploring students' understanding of complex arguments and controversial points of views. For example, as part of a conservation study, to assess understanding and attitudes, a student could be asked to take on the role of a bird lover who wants to save a particular endangered species. Another student could be asked to take on the role of a logger who wants to fell the trees in a part of the forest where the endangered species lives. The rest of the students become "interviewers." They research the topic, perhaps working collaboratively, and come up with some good questions to put to the bird lover and the logger.

Another possible variation on the in-role interview is for the teacher to be interviewed in-role. If you do this, a simple prop such as a pair of glasses or a hat is a useful way to signal to the students when you are being the teacher and when you're in-role.

The activity continues with the interviewee being interviewed. The dramatic frame for this activity can be made even more complex by giving the interviewers a "role." For example, you might announce that the interviewers are reporters from rival newspapers or rival radio stations. The reporters then have to "phone in" their stories to their editors. The rest of the class listens while they call on an imaginary telephone and dictate what they know and what they think about the interviewee.

The teacher then records significant assessment data in some form of anecdotal notebook, file, or record card.

Freeze frame

Main assessment strategy: Re-creation
Other strategies: Interaction and Observation

This is an interesting and useful extension of re-creating a learning experience by dramatization. One of the main challenges encountered in dramatization, or "acting out" an experience, is discovering how to coordinate what it feels like from the inside with what the dramatization looks like from the outside. The freeze frame device allows students to explore both viewpoints.

The teacher sets up the dramatic activity but tells the students that from time to time they will "still" the action by calling out, "Freeze." While activity is in "freeze frame," the observing students and the teacher comment and discuss the implications of what is happening and make suggestions for what might happen next. The participants can also be questioned and can choose to reply as themselves or in-role. They can also step out of the freeze frame so they can see what it looks like from the outside. Everyone is encouraged to express their thoughts and feelings and to "try out" ideas. The teacher facilitates and assists by questioning and probing the students' perceptions and understanding.

For assessment purposes, the teacher records any significant data on the students' knowledge and understanding, their skills and strategies, and their attitudes and values in some form of anecdotal notebook, file, or card system.

Action replay

Main assessment strategy: Re-creation
Other strategies: Interaction and Observation

Like the freeze frame, the action replay is an extension of dramatization. When a group of students is presenting a dramatization of a story or an event, the teacher and observing students can ask the performers to stop and replay a sequence. There can also be some discussion and suggestions as to alternative ways the event or story could be presented or developed.

For example, with a dramatization of the story of *The Three Billy Goats Gruff*, the teacher might facilitate a replay of the bridge crossing. What might have happened if, instead of the littlest billy goat, the biggest billy goat had gone first? Or what if all three had gone together? Or what if they had tried to negotiate with the troll–maybe offering him some goats' hair so he could knit himself a sweater in return for a safe crossing?

While facilitating these replays, the teacher observes and interacts with the students. Significant assessment data is recorded in some form of anecdotal notebook, file, or record card.

Tableaux

Main assessment strategy: Re-creation
Other strategies: Interaction and Observation

The purpose of this activity is to make a "living photograph." The tableaux device is useful in assessing student understanding and attitudes in the study of literature, historical events, and the social sciences. For example, a teacher might facilitate the creation of a tableaux after reading a story. Through discussion, a significant "scene" is chosen. The teacher then works with the students to re-create the scene in tableaux form.

For example, students in a first grade classroom might depict a scene in tableaux form from *Where the Wild Things Are*, by Maurice Sendak. The class could choose the part in the story where Max says good-bye to the Wild Things. Children would be chosen to be Max and the monsters–but this wouldn't be "acting" in the usual sense of the word, because in a tableaux their role is largely "pictorial." As each new person is added to the picture, another student is chosen to be the "director" and decide how and where the person will appear.

As the teacher facilitates the creation of the tableaux, he or she also observes and interacts with the students and, in so doing, assesses the students' understanding and response to the learning experiences. Significant data is recorded in some form of anecdotal notebook, file, or record card. It might also be a useful idea to have the observing students do a quick sketch of the tableau or for the teacher to take a photograph of it. The sketches or photograph can be used subsequently for a review of the learning.

Assessment Tools That Facilitate Reflection

Self-portraits

Main assessment strategy: Reflection
Other strategies: Interaction and Observation

As the teacher, have your students create a head-and-shoulders self-portrait for a class Self-Portrait Exhibition. Then have each student write an "autobiographical note" for the exhibition catalog. It will help if you issue some guidelines for this activity. The following is a sample list of such guidelines.

Information you might like to include in your catalog note about yourself:

your name (Of course!)
the names of your family members and your pets
your favorite color, food, TV show, and computer game
your favorite book or story
your favorite writer
what you like to do in your spare time
your greatest claim to fame so far
the person you admire most in the world, and why
the most wonderful thing that has happened to you in your life so far
any special goals you hope to achieve in the near future

This catalog material is drafted and revised. After it has been edited, it is assembled in the finished exhibition catalog. You might want to enter the information in a computer file and print out an official-looking version to be displayed with the exhibition or distributed to classroom visitors.

The self-portraits should be displayed in the classroom for a period of time, and then should be taken down and assembled into a class big book. The autobiographical notes can be attached next to the students' self-portrait. It might be fun to revisit these autobiographical notes later in the year and write an update.

Throughout this activity, the teacher observes and reflects on the students and notes significant assessment data in an anecdotal notebook, file, or record card.

Peer portraits

Main assessment Strategy: Reflection
Other strategies: Interaction and Observation

In creating peer portraits, the students work together in pairs. Each student has a large piece of light cardboard that is larger than the size of the child. One student lies on the cardboard while the other student draws an outline of his or her form. Each then completes a full-length portrait of the other, trying to make it as accurate and lifelike as possible. The portrait is then cut out and turned over.

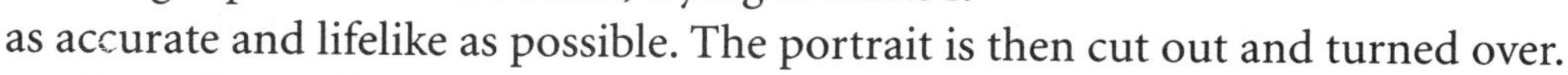

Then the students interview each other and try to find out as much interesting information as they can about each other–interests, likes and dislikes, hobbies, favorite books, favorite foods, colors, and TV shows, what they enjoy about school, what they don't enjoy, where they live, what pets they have, what their bedroom is like, etc. All the information the subject is happy to be made public is recorded on the back of the portrait. The aim of this activity is to make a "positive word portrait"–to find out enough positive and interesting information to completely cover one side of the portrait.

An entertaining way to present these portraits is for the artists to hold the portraits in front of them and read out the notes as if they are the person: *"Hi, I'm Danziel, and I came from Poland. My favorite color..."*

To display a Peer Portrait, attach a string to the top of the "head" and hang it so it can be turned around and read.

Throughout this activity, the teacher observes and interacts with the students. Significant assessment data is recorded in an anecdotal notebook, file, or record card.

Teacher's confidential file

Main assessment strategy: Reflection
Additional strategy: Observation

Teachers need a file they can refer to for key information about each student. Usually schools and school districts mandate their own documents, but if this is not the case in your district or school, you might want to use or adapt the form on the next page.

Confidential File

Personal Information	
Name:	
Likes to be called:	
Parent/s' or Guardian's name/s:	
Home address:	
Work address:	
Home telephone:	Daytime telephone number, if different:
Fax:	E-mail address:
Date of birth:	Age:
Emergency Information	
Emergency contacts (include names, addresses, telephone numbers):	
Family Information	
Any brothers or sisters?	
Names (if attending this school, which room/grade/teacher):	
Position in family:	
Other significant family information:	
Health Information	
Medical problems:	
Allergies:	
Regular medications:	
Family doctor or medical clinic:	
Sight tested? When? OK?	
Hearing tested? When? OK?	
Other health notes:	
Other Significant Information	
Review Dates	
Checked after one month. Date:	
Checked after six months. Date:	
Checked after nine months. Date:	
(Enter dates in calendar to prompt future reviews)	

All about me

Main assessment strategy: Reflection

In addition to the teacher's confidential files, it can be very useful for both student and teacher if the students prepare their own "files," or "personal dossiers." The "All About Me" form is a useful example; however, you might want to adapt this form to your class, or better still, use it as a starting point and have your students help you devise your own "All About Me" form.

All About Me
Stuff I Want My Teacher to Know about Me
My name:
What I like to be called:
When my birthday is (I'm expecting you to remember it!):
How I get to school:
How I usually go home from school:
Secret stuff I want only my teacher to know:
Some Special Things about Me
Three things I like to do when I have spare time:
1.
2.
3.
Some books I like people to read to me:
Some books I like to read by myself:
Things I like to draw:
Things I like to write about:
Things I like to daydream about:
What I like to watch on TV or video:
Do I have a computer I can use at home? Yes No

If yes, what are some of the things I like to do on my computer?
These are some of my favorite things (favorite color, TV show, time of day, pet, person):
Other special things I want my teacher to know about me:
Any goals or things I'd like to do or achieve in this grade/class:
Things I'd like to be able to do or do better:
These are some of the things I like to do (cross out the things that don't apply): giggle, listen to music, draw pictures, watch TV, play computer games, talk to friends, smile, play a musical instrument, listen to stories, make up jokes, play games, listen to jokes, help others, laugh at funny things, cry at sad things, swim, ride my bike, make things out of wood and other stuff, clean up my room, make my own inventions, visit my grandmother and grandfather, sing, and think of smart things to say.
Other things I like to do:
Important. This file was last updated (date):

My computer dossier

Main assessment strategy: Reflection
Other strategies: Interaction and Observation

If you have computers in your classroom, it is a good idea for each student to have an individual file that can be used as a kind of "computer portfolio." Provided the students don't object to their portfolios being available to anyone else, these could be kept on the hard drive. More personal or confidential data could be kept on a student's own floppy disk. Such a dossier could include stories they have word processed, their "All About Me" file, and any letters they have written. If they have an Internet connection, they can also include copies of any E-mail messages they've sent and received, along with their favorite

Internet links and sites.

From time to time, the students could select from the dossier the material they would be happy to share and give this to you as a file or printout. You might like to use the material for a conference with the student. In addition, you could note significant assessment data in an anecdotal notebook, file, or record card.

Student autobiographies

Main assessment strategy:	Reflection
Other strategies:	Interaction and Observation

Encourage your students to write their own autobiographies. These can be multi-chaptered volumes–perhaps with a chapter per year. The students could interview relatives and family friends for a section called, "Things my family and other relatives remember about me." They might want to include photocopies of photographs of themselves as babies and toddlers, too. Their school years could include material from fellow students and past teachers, plus highlights of the class program.

By its very nature, an autobiography requires considerable personal reflection. The finished autobiography could also spark valuable student/teacher and student/student discussion and interaction. This could also be an ongoing activity, with new chapters being added as the child progresses from one grade to the next.

"Who am I?" partner interviews

Main assessment strategy:	Reflection
Other strategies:	Interaction and Observation

This is a simple device that often yields valuable insight into student learning and student attitudes and beliefs. It's also an enjoyable writing activity that helps the students get to know one another (while helping the teacher to get to know them, too).

The students choose or are assigned a partner. The partners should be students who don't know each other very well, as opposed to being "best friends." Together, they brainstorm and list "respectful" questions they could ask each other–ones the other student would feel at ease answering. As they complete each question, they write it again in large writing and give it to the teacher, who glues or pins it to a large sheet of paper headed:

Our Class Question Pile
Are any of these of use to you?

These help provide models for students and also assist students who are having difficulty coming up with appropriate questions. It also provides an opportunity for the teacher to help where necessary with editing.

When the students have brainstormed sufficiently, each one chooses a number of questions (seven, say) that they think will provide the most interesting information. They copy these onto a special questionnaire form, leaving sufficient space between the questions for the answers. The next stage is the interview, which is often best left to another day or time.

The students interview their partners and complete the questionnaire, but instead of mentioning their names, they use an agreed upon "code name." They write their code names next to their real names on a mail label, which is then given to the teacher to paste in a special little notebook with the heading:

Our Class Secret Code Book

The finished questionnaires are displayed, and students are encouraged to read them and try to guess who the person is being interviewed. Then they write their guesses, along with the reasons for their assumptions, on slips of paper and attach them to the questionnaires. *("I think this is Gwenda because ....")*

After a period of days, the teacher finally displays the code book so the children can check their hunches. Meanwhile, the teacher reads all the student responses and records any significant data in an anecdotal notebook, file, or record card.

The questionnaires can eventually be taken down from the display and turned into a class big book, with the code names listed in the back. The big book can then be loaned to other classes so that other students can take part in the guessing game. If more than one class has done this exercise, it is fun to exchange "Who Am I?" books.

Personal journals

Main assessment strategy: Reflection
Additional strategy: Artifact Collection

In using this device, the students keep a personal journal in which they write about themselves, their work at school, their thoughts and feelings, their goals and aspirations, their hopes and daydreams, and their worries and concerns.

The best way to encourage students to do this is for the teacher to model it. Set aside a period of time each day to help your students get into the routine of keeping a personal journal. Write with them–publicly–on large sheets of paper or overhead transparencies. It helps to set a focus for each day's writing: Begin your piece with an introductory phrase that indicates the focus. For example:

Today I want to write about how I felt when I received a letter from a friend whom I haven't seen for years and years.

Or:

Today I want to write about the new goal I have set for myself. I have decided I really have to learn more about using the computer.

It is important that personal journals remain personal and, therefore, private. However, you might also encourage your students to read segments of their journals–to friends, family members, the teacher, or their classmates–if they feel comfortable doing so. This can be encouraged by asking at the end of each personal journal writing session, "Does anyone have anything they want to share with the class?"

The teacher then records any significant data in an anecdotal notebook, file, or record card.

Goal setting

Main assessment strategy: Reflection
Additional strategy: Interaction

It is a good idea to encourage personal goal setting.

The student spends some time listing a small number of goals. It is important not to have too many (three goals, or even just one, is fine). Goals should be challenging, but also realistic and attainable. The following "Goal Checklist" might be helpful.

Checklist for my personal Goals

1. ***Do I have any goals?***
   If you don't have any goals of your own, you tend to end up having to try to meet the goals other people set for you.
2. ***Am I sure they really are goals?***
   Goals are things we really want to achieve. Things you'd like to be able to do aren't goals–they're just nice ideas. A goal has to be something you feel strongly about. It's something you HAVE to do!

3. ***Do I have too many goals?***
When you have too many goals you're inclined to lose sight of some of them. One goal is fine. Three is OK. Having more than three is dangerous!
4. ***Am I sure my goals are realistic? Do I have a chance of achieving them?***
It's easy to get discouraged if you set out to try to do the impossible. It's fine having as your goal to be able to fly like a bird if you are a chick; but if you're an elephant, you're probably not going to make it!
5. ***Have I written my goals in my own words?***
If you have them written down, you're not likely to forget them.
6. ***How often do I remind myself of my goals?***
It's a good idea to remind yourself what your goals are regularly–such as every day–and at a special time of the day–such as breakfast, or before going to sleep.
7. ***Do I have any personal heroes who have achieved their goals?***
Sometimes other people's achievements can spur us on. They don't even have to share our goals. It's the example they set that is helpful.
8. ***Have I told anyone what my goals are?***
Sometimes sharing your goals with your friends or your teacher or your family is useful because they might be able to help you achieve them.
9. ***Do I keep a record of how close I am getting to achieving my goals?***
Keeping track can help you stay motivated.
10. ***Do I praise myself when I do something that helps me get closer to achieving my goals?***
The best applause is your own applause!

Student "Things I Know and Can Do" log

Main assessment strategy:	Observation
Other strategies:	Reflection and Interaction
You will need:	A "Things I know and Can Do" log sheet for each student

Prepare a "Things I Know and Can Do" log sheet for each student. Then encourage your students to regularly enter things they can do, things they need to know more about, and things they need help with in their log sheets.

The best way to make this device work is for the teacher to model it by keeping his or her own "Things I Know and Can Do" log, and maybe displaying it or keeping it where the students can read it. It helps to regularly set aside a few minutes each week for making log entries. Seeing the teacher keeping a log up-to-date is not only a great reminder but also a great source of encouragement to do likewise.

You might like to use this as an assessment tool for all subject areas, as in the example below. It is also possible to use the same device for one particular subject area, such as writing. In this case, the heading would be: "Things I know and Can Do in Writing." Use the same format as in the example, but delete the subject column.

Encourage your students to bring their logs with them when they want to have a student/teacher conference, or when the teacher wants to have a teacher/student conference!

Name: ______________________________ Things I Know and Can Do Log

Things I know about or can do:	Date:	Subject this is useful for:
Butterflies	*9/24*	*Science*
Multiplying by 5	*10/7*	*Math*
Exclamation marks	*10/9*	*Writing*
Space shuttles	*10/23*	*Science*

Things I need to know more about or need help with:	Date:	Subject:
Use quotation marks when I am writing	*9/21*	*Writing*
Volcanoes	*10/29*	*Science and writing*

My art dossier

Main assessment strategy: Reflection
Additional strategy: Artifact Collection

On the surface, this looks like a tool for helping students reflect on their work in art. But in practice, if the art reflects their learning and growth in other areas of their lives, it can provide valuable insights into other aspects of their learning and life experiences.

When the students complete a piece of art of any kind, have them complete a "My Art Dossier" form. This involves sketching a small cartoon version of their work as a reminder of what it was about and then completing some responses, as in the example on the following page.

The form is then filed–a ring binder works well–and over time, accumulated examples begin to provide a fascinating commentary and narrative.

My Art Dossier

<table>
<tr><td>What it looked like:
(Quick cartoon sketch only)</td><td>TITLE: What I called it.</td></tr>
<tr><td rowspan="3"></td><td>PURPOSE: Why I created it.</td></tr>
<tr><td>MATERIALS: What materials did I use?</td></tr>
<tr><td>TECHNIQUES: What art techniques did I use?</td></tr>
<tr><td colspan="2">IDEAS: What was I thinking about while I was doing it?</td></tr>
<tr><td colspan="2">FEELINGS: How was I feeling while I worked on it?</td></tr>
<tr><td colspan="2">CONNECTIONS: Did it make me think of anything else I have done or seen or felt?</td></tr>
<tr><td colspan="2">AND? Anything else I want to add.</td></tr>
</table>

Things I want to write about

Main assessment strategy: Reflection
Additional strategy: Observation

It is helpful to encourage your students to think about topics and ideas they might like to write about as part of their preparation for writing. They can build up their own personal lists of topics and think about them long before they actually begin to put words on paper. The very act of preparing such a list and keeping it current is a valuable reflective activity that encourages students to take stock of their personal experiences, interests, and areas of writing expertise.

Such a list might look something like the chart on the next page.

Things I Want to Write About

Topics, ideas, types of writing (poems, stories, articles, etc.), mood.	Date I first thought of this	Date I started writing this	Date I finished this piece
Article about frogs	9/4	9/18	9/22
Guided tour of my bedroom	9/7	9/30	10/4
Poem about my favorite food	9/13		
Spooky horror story	10/24	10/29	
How to care for pet lizards	10/28		
Story gran told me about the war	11/4		

Personal video log

Main assessment strategy: Reflection
Additional strategy: Observation

If a student has access to a videocamera (at home or at school), then a video log is an interesting and novel way to keep a personal record of the things the student has done, experienced, and learned. The student keeps a videocassette for this purpose, and whenever some significant piece of work has been completed, he or she videotapes it while providing a voice-over commentary, giving the date, what the work involved, and why the student has decided to keep a video record of it. The personal video can also be taken home and shared with the student's family.

As the teacher, you might like to model this activity by keeping your own personal video log of the teaching year. It is important to keep the segments short so that watching the tape doesn't become a tedious exercise. Actually, from an assessment point of view, the most significant part of this activity is the reflection involved in the preparation of the commentary.

This activity also works well in a "buddy" situation where the students work in pairs to help each other prepare their personal video logs. In this case, the buddy videotapes the student who shows the work and talks to the camera.

"How I Feel About" checklists

Main assessment strategy: Reflection
Additional strategy: Observation

This activity uses the "Plus, Minus, and Interesting" framework developed by Edward de Bono. The students list topics and then give reactions in three different ways–what they like or liked about the topic, what they don't or didn't like about it, and what they find or found interesting about it. This is a very useful way to have students evaluate a topic or segment of work, but it can also be used to evaluate a subject area, a term's work, or a school of personal experience. It encourages students to change viewpoints and to evaluate their own feelings and responses. It can be used as a one off activity to evaluate a particular topic, or it can be used as an accumulating document.

Needless to say, the student's reflections can be significant to the teacher, too.

A "How I Feel About" checklist might look something like this:

How I Feel About

Topic/Subject	Plus	Minus	Interesting
A trip to the zoo.	The monkeys. The lions eating. Filling out our information sheets. Having lunch together by the birds.	The bus ride–it was hot! The crocodile was scary.	What the zoo lady told us about the crocodile's teeth. The animals in the cages–did they want to get out?

My "Eurekas!"

Main assessment strategy: Reflection
Additional strategy: Observation

Eureka was the word Archimedes was reputed to have shouted when he discovered the principle of displacement while slipping into his bath–a principle that would enable him to measure the purity of gold and solve the problem the king was having with his crooked jewelers. Apparently Archimedes was so excited by the discovery that he jumped from his bath and ran unclothed through the streets, shouting "Eureka! I have it!"

One of the exciting things about being a learner is that exhilarating moment when suddenly, for the first time, a student makes a connection between experiences and comes to the startling realization that he or she has discovered or grasped or invented a new idea! This activity is a way to help students celebrate and reflect on those moments.

The students keep their own personal lists in which they enter the details of such discoveries. Also, at a regular time each week, the teacher gives the students an opportunity to share any of their "eurekas" with the class. Of course, the teacher can share his or her eurekas, too.

This activity encourages students to really value their learning experiences and cherish the excitement of thinking, creative problem solving, and the wonder of new ideas.

(See the sample "Eureka" list below.)

My "Eurekas!"

Where was I?	What was I doing at the time?	What was my Eureka?
I was in the art room.	I was coloring my picture with a yellow crayon and some of the yellow went on my blue sky.	It turned green. When you put yellow over blue, it turns into green!

Assessment Tools That Facilitate Simulation

Standardized tests

Main assessment strategy: Simulation
Additional strategy: Interaction

We have criticized the use made of standardized tests in a number of places in this book. However, it is important to make it clear that the problem is not so much with the tests themselves but the ways they have been interpreted and used in the traditional classroom. It's not that we think standardized tests should be banned, but rather that they should be used only where they are appropriate and helpful–where they help our students to learn more effectively.

Standardized tests do have some valuable uses. Group tests, for example, provide useful data for making tentative determinations about group issues such as broad funding decisions and large group accountability matters. But it isn't appropriate to try to apply group data when trying to decide the specific learning needs of individuals and small, classroom-size groups.

One of the criticisms of mass testing is that it disrupts the learning program. But there are ways of reducing these problems. One way is to limit the survey to a representative sample rather than test an entire population. Another is to survey only particular age or grade levels so that students have to encounter the test situation periodically–say every three years. Mass group testing of the very young should be avoided anyway, partly because of problems with reliability and interpretation, but also because there are simpler and better ways to assess learning.

Intensive one-on-one standardized tests for individual diagnosis of special educational needs also have their place, provided they are used in conjunction with a range of other assessment strategies such as observation, interaction, re-creation, reflection, and learning artifact collection.

Teacher-made tests

Main assessment strategy:	Simulation
Other strategies:	Observation and Interaction

Teacher-made tests can be used as a quick shortcut to check on students' knowledge, understanding, skills, and strategies. We can ask them what they know to test their knowledge; or give them problems to solve to check on their understanding or their ability to use learned skills and strategies; or we can ask them to show what they think, feel, or believe to check on their attitudes and values.

We are so used to using tests in the school environment that we seldom think very closely about how well we use them or how appropriate they are for what we need to know. The following are "handy hints" to bear in mind when using teacher-made tests to assess learning.

1. We should be sure we need to test. Are there other ways we can gather the same information that might, in fact, be easier and more empowering to the learner? What about observation? What about interaction? What about asking the learners to reflect and tell us themselves?
2. We should be very clear about what the test is actually testing and what the results really tell us. A test usually involves sampling and generalizing–we test the students on a sample of the learning and then

we generalize from their test results and say those results probably indicate how well the students have mastered all the learning. But, in fact, it is in both these crucial steps that tests are just as likely to "get it wrong." For example, to find out how well students are likely to spell when writing, we might choose to test them on a list of high-frequency words. Our sampling could be inappropriate because the spelling words might not be the words the students want to use when writing. Our generalizing could be inappropriate, too, because the students might not feel motivated to spell accurately when they are working on a list of words, whereas they might be more careful when they're writing about a subject to which they feel committed. In fact, all we can really say with confidence about the test results is that they show how well a student can spell a list of words.

3. It is also important to make sure the test not only assesses the learning but also assists, or at least doesn't deter, the learner. We want to challenge and motivate our students, not crush and crucify them.
4. However, having said that, we also need to have high expectations for our students. If we really want them to learn, we do have to keep pushing them to the frontiers of their learning. Empowered learners enjoy being "tested" in all the positive senses of that word. In fact, they might enjoy testing themselves.
5. Beware of constructing tests where the overriding consideration is making them easy to mark. Multiple-choice tests are much-loved by teachers for this very reason, but their validity and thus, their instructional usefulness, might be seriously limited by the mechanics of the multiple-choice format.
6. We should be wary of always constructing test questions where there is an obvious single correct answer. To encourage creative thinking and sophisticated problem solving, it is valuable to have questions for which a range of answers is possible, or where the unexpected answer might be the best one. We don't always want what is "correct"–we also want ideas that are imaginative, innovative, surprising, and original.
7. We should be wary of relying solely on the question/answer type test format, where the student can only respond within the narrow confines of the test maker's questions. Students also need open-ended type tests where they have an opportunity to expand on an idea, develop a theme, or construct an argument.
8. The teacher doesn't always have to be the one asking the questions! When we encourage students to construct their own tests, the questions they choose to ask will often give us a different and meaningful insight into their grasp and understanding of the material.

It might also give students greater ownership of their own learning. The test becomes less of a threatening experience and more of an enjoyable quiz or a game.

9. The teacher doesn't always have to be the one who marks the test. Deciding on appropriate criteria and then letting the students assess their own learning helps them internalize the assessment process. In this way, the test doesn't just assess the learning; it becomes part of the learning process, too.
10. Tests don't always need to be solo exercises for the student. For some kinds of learning, it is best if the test experience is a collaborative one.

Testing in pairs

Main assessment strategy: Simulation
Other strategies: Interaction and Observation

For many activities, it is helpful to encourage students to test each other. Personal spelling lists, for example, are excellent opportunities for this type of testing. After a brief, intensive "learning" session of about five minutes, the students ask their buddies to "test" them and initial and date their personal spelling notebooks for each word spelled correctly and without hesitation. The personal spelling list on the following page includes columns for a buddy test, a teacher test, and a parent test. Students are tested in this order to try to ensure that the spelling test with the parent is a positive experience for the child.

Testing in pairs is an excellent review activity for use in other areas of the curriculum, too. After a science lesson, for example, you might ask your students to find a buddy and have them ask each other some good questions about the session. The students pair test scores are not necessarily recorded, but the teacher can record significant anecdotal information.

This is a useful way to review the day, too. Just before going home, students pair up and ask each other questions about what they did during the day. It is valuable to do something like this at the end of the day because it will still be fresh in the students' minds when they are greeted by their parents with the inevitable question: "What did you do at school today?"

The words I need to learn	Buddy test	Teacher test	Parent test
house	2/7 BJ	2/9	2/11
havoc	2/8 BJ	2/10	2/12
ocean	2/12 BJ	2/14	
swimming	2/14 BJ		
hurricane	2/15 BJ		

Socio-graphs

Main assessment strategy: Simulation
Additional strategy: Interaction

To lay out the mechanics first: the teacher explains that, for some of the activities the class will be conducting during the year, it will be helpful to have some idea as to who each student would prefer to be working with. The teacher then gives out slips of paper and asks the students to put their own names on the paper first, and then write down the names of two people they would pick to work with if they could–a first choice and a second choice. The teacher explains that this information will be completely confidential and then collects the pieces of paper when the students have finished.

Later the teacher begins to illustrate the information graphically, linking the students to their first choice with arrows of one color (red, say), and linking them to their second choice with arrows of another color (green). Once all the information has been recorded in this way, the teacher counts how many times each student has been chosen by someone. A new socio-graph is now prepared, with the most frequently chosen students in the middle. The resulting picture is then studied and the teacher attempts to find any important factors or implications for instruction in the social information. For example, it might be that the most popular students show potential leadership qualities, while isolated students–those whom no one has chosen–might need support and help with social skills.

A word of warning: as with all assessments based on simulation, we need to undertake such speculation with caution. Being "isolated" could, in fact, be an indication that the student is strong enough and self-valuing enough not to need the popularity and adulation of the group. At the same time, the popularity of one student might tell us more about the insecurity or immaturity of the group of admirers!

The most valid and helpful assessment of personal confidence and social skills comes from observing our students in real social experiences rather than from hypothetical and simulated situations. In other words, the brief snapshot provided by a socio-graph should be used only as a quick "first sketch" and a prelude to regular sympathetic and sensitive "kidwatching."

Assessment Tools That Facilitate Artifact Collection

Learner-managed learning portfolios

Main assessment strategy: Artifact Collection
Other strategies: Reflection and Interaction

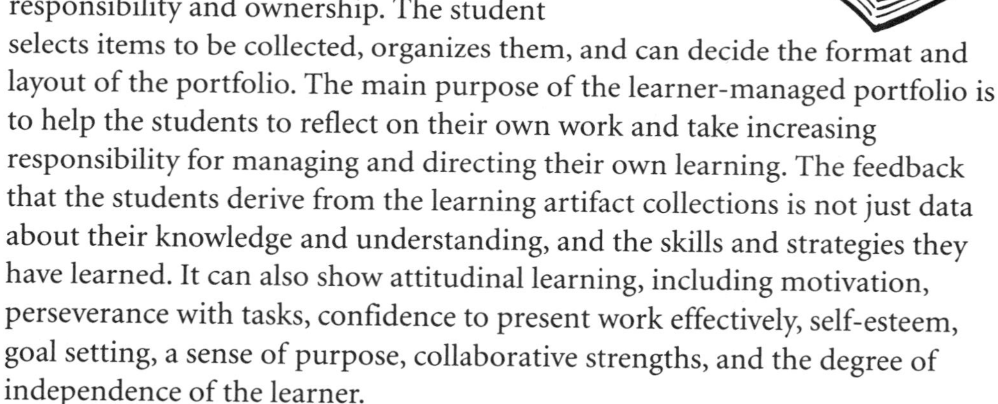

There are many ways in which portfolios can be organized, managed, "owned," and used. A learner-managed learning portfolio is one in which the student has the prime responsibility and ownership. The student selects items to be collected, organizes them, and can decide the format and layout of the portfolio. The main purpose of the learner-managed portfolio is to help the students to reflect on their own work and take increasing responsibility for managing and directing their own learning. The feedback that the students derive from the learning artifact collections is not just data about their knowledge and understanding, and the skills and strategies they have learned. It can also show attitudinal learning, including motivation, perseverance with tasks, confidence to present work effectively, self-esteem, goal setting, a sense of purpose, collaborative strengths, and the degree of independence of the learner.

Learner-managed portfolios provide excellent opportunities for students to demonstrate their own creative flair and ingenuity, and they can be remarkably diverse. From the teacher's point of view, this sometimes makes the learner-managed portfolio a little challenging. The following checklist should help teachers to assist their students in making some of the key decisions necessary for the introduction and management of learner portfolios.

Portfolio checklist

Format: Will it be a book? Scrapbook? Notebook? Photo album? Ring binder? Box? File? File with plastic sleeves? Computer file? Filing cabinet file? Envelope? Wall hanging with plastic pockets? Plastic bag on hangers? Video portfolio?

Contents: Will it include writing samples? Art samples? Project samples? Photographs? A journal? Reflective pieces? Reading log? Writing log? Mathematics log? Video log? Audio tapes? Pieces by other students about the learner? Pieces by the parents about the learner? All about me? "I can do" lists for: reading, writing, spelling, mathematics, social studies, science, or information technology?

Management: Will the students select all the pieces on their own? Will they select some and the teacher select others? Will they select the pieces according to prescribed teacher-set or school-set requirements?

Will the students assemble their portfolios on their own time, or during class time? Will there be a date on which the portfolios will be checked by the teacher?

Will the portfolios be kept at school, or will the students be able to take them home for their parents to see?

What will happen at the end of the year? Will the portfolios be kept at school by the teacher, or taken home by the students to keep? Or will they grow with the students through the grades and be taken home when the children leave the school? Or will the school take a videotape copy of the material in the portfolio at the end of the year for record purposes so the students can take their portfolios home?

Use: Will the portfolios be used to document learning? Will they include only the best pieces or finished work as "show" portfolios? Or will they include works in progress to illustrate process as "working" portfolios? Will they be used as a focus for regular student/teacher conferences? Will they be used as a focus for three-way conferences involving student, parent, and teacher?

Portfolio handy hints

1. All items should be dated so that we know when the learning happened and can start to see sequence and progress.
2. A note should be attached to each item, explaining why it was selected. For kindergarten children, the notes can be written by the teacher. Older children can write their own notes, although it sometimes helps to make up a little form they can complete so as to prompt them to do this.
3. Portfolios should be regularly checked by the teacher–preferably with the student acting as a "guide." It is helpful to draw up a schedule for these conferences.
4. Portfolios should have an index or table of contents so that people can find their way around the material and parents and teachers can see at a glance what is included.

5. It helps students to structure their portfolios if the teacher sets some minimum requirements, or if the teacher and the student decide on those requirements collaboratively. Extra items can always be added, but it assists students with planning and goal setting if they have some idea of what they need to do first.
6. The best way to promote portfolios is to share them. Set aside regular periods for students to share their portfolios with their classmates–or with students from other grades.
7. "Portfolio buddies" is a great idea to try, but rather than pairing students at the same grade level, it might be interesting to pair them at different levels. For example, you might pair a first grade student with a third-grader. Both students have the responsibility of sharing their portfolios with each other and helping each other. The third-grader becomes a kind of mentor to the first grade student, while the younger child can become a great "fan" and motivator of the older student.
8. Even though the students will be selecting work for their portfolios, the teacher can still influence this process by prompting and highlighting student examples. *"Girls and boys, I'd like you all to check out Deena's portfolio sometime. She's got a great comic book sketch that shows how she completed her science project."* (The teacher's message is really, *"Have you thought about using a comic storyboard to plot your science project learning?"*)
9. The best way to encourage student portfolios is for the teacher to keep a personal portfolio and share the process of organizing, formatting, and managing it with the students.

Teacher-managed learning portfolios

Main assessment strategy: Artifact Collection
Other strategies: Reflection and Interaction

Teacher-managed portfolios are similar to the learner-managed variety, except that the teacher makes most of the key decisions regarding selection and organization. This can make this type of portfolio a little more uniform and perhaps a little easier to manage from the teacher's point of view. Teachers can select materials to document learning growth throughout the year and usually pass this accumulated material on to next year's teachers (after culling surplus material in the process to ensure that the portfolios are of a manageable size). The down side is that, because the students do not have ownership, teacher-managed portfolios might be less exciting or motivating for them.

One useful approach is to have both systems running side by side. The students keep their own full portfolio as described earlier, but the teacher also keeps a more skeletal portfolio that is more closely tailored to provide data on the planned learning outcomes.

The use of original work can be an issue: teachers should ask their students' permission to keep pieces of work in their portfolios. (It's a matter of acknowledging the students' ownership of the learning, although usually, the students are flattered!) If your students want to keep their own work or use it in their own portfolios, then a photocopy will suffice.

Video portfolios

Main assessment strategy: Artifact Collection
Other strategies: Reflection and Interaction

A video portfolio can be a simple and highly portable way to record student learning. The teacher keeps a videotape for each student in the class. Written and visual material can be videotaped while the teacher and/or learner uses a voice-over to provide the date, the context for the learning, and the reasons why it was selected.

One of the big advantages of this kind of portfolio is the ability to capture aspects of learning that are not readily discernible from work on paper. Skills can be captured and performances can be recorded. The master tape can be copied for the students to take home and share with their families. The students can also create graphics to signal where each child appears in the video and create full tables of contents to assist viewers who wish to watch selected segments.

Reading logs

Main assessment strategy: Artifact Collection
Other strategies: Reflection and Interaction

Encouraging students to keep a log of their reading is not only helpful to them–as their log grows, it gives them a sense of accomplishment–but it also provides valuable information for the teacher. The number of books shows how much independent reading the student is doing as well as the kinds of books, their level of difficulty, subject, length, and genre.

It is possible to make these logs more interactive, too–as in the example on the next page.

Title	Author	Date started	Date finished	Would I recommend it to someone?	Why?	People I have recommended it to
Charlotte's Web		9/11	9/19	Yes	You have to keep reading to find out what's going to happen. Also I liked the pig!	Sandra, Toni, Dad. My big sister has already read it.
CHECK						

Mini time capsules

Main assessment strategy: Artifact Collection
Other strategies: Reflection and Interaction

In using this assessment tool, the teacher explains to the students at the start of the year that the class is going to prepare a mini time capsule–it's only a "mini" time capsule because they will be keeping it for just one year. The aim is to collect as many things as possible that will provide a kind of snapshot of the class–who they are, what they can do, what their interests are, and where they think they are going. At the end of the year, the students open up the time capsule again to see how much they have changed and grown , and how much they have stayed the same. The following is a checklist of things you might like to include in your mini time capsule. The students could provide:

Self-portraits
Their age
Their height
The number of teeth they have (if kindergarten or first grade)
Their favorites (favorite color, food, hobby, interest, TV show, movie, game, book, author, singer or singing group, musical instrument, etc.)
Goals, dreams, and aspirations
Worries and concerns

Completing Our Learning Assessment Plan

Now that we have thought about the strategies and assessment tools we think we will use, we can add these to our Learning Assessment Plan. Of course, we can change and modify these as the year unfolds and as we respond to our students' learning. Right now, we're ready to start teaching and start putting them into practice! That's what the next chapter is all about. But before we do that, maybe you'd like to complete the "What Have I Done?" checklist.

Chapter Review: The "What Have I Done?" Checklist

The "What Have I Done?" Checklist

Instructions:

Read the following items carefully and place a check mark √ next to the things you've done with this chapter.

- ❑ Read it from the first word, which is *Chapter*, to the last word, which is *this.*
- ❑ Thought about it.
- ❑ Told someone else about it.
- ❑ Turned my nose up at parts of it.
- ❑ Had an argument with myself over some parts of it.
- ❑ Had an argument with the author about some parts.
- ❑ Read half of it and wondered what I could have for dinner.
- ❑ Wondered how all of this would work with my class.
- ❑ Wondered if the principal would let me do this with my class.
- ❑ Wondered how I could keep my principal from finding out when I do this with my class.
- ❑ Wondered how the teachers at my school are going to react when I tell them they all have to do this.

Chapter 5

Getting Started

The Year Begins: All Systems Go!

In This Chapter

So, Now We're Ready to Start

We've planned the learning, and we've planned how we intend to assess it. We might have done all this on our own because everyone else in the school just wants to go on doing what they've always been doing. (Some people just never bother to fix something because they haven't realized it's broken!) Right now, we're feeling pretty good because we're all set to make it work in our own classrooms. Ah, the empowering pleasure of doing your own thing!

Or we might have worked on this collaboratively as a faculty and prepared a learning assessment plan for the whole school. We've got a strong team feeling going here! Haven't we done well?

Or we might have managed to get the whole school district to work on this project! Quite a circus, in fact! And now we're all feeling very proud of ourselves. Hey, we're becoming a learning community! (OK, so we had an argument or two on some issues, but that was really very healthy because it helped us straighten out our thinking on some pretty basic beliefs as to how children learn and how we can best facilitate that learning.)

Regardless of how we arrived at this point, here we are, poised on the edge of the diving board and just about to take the plunge!

But wait! We still have some things to think about!

1. We have to be able to *record* our assessments. We need to know how to use the Learning Assessment Plan for this purpose.
2. Then we have to plan the *time frame* for our assessments and make up a schedule that shows when we are going to do what.
3. To help us do this, we'll need some *prompts* to make sure we keep to our *schedule* and to ensure that we assess and evaluate the whole learning spectrum without leaving anything out or spending too much time on some areas and neglecting learning growth in others.
4. And before we get too carried away with *our* problems and tasks, we need to remember what we learned from our Assessment Audit back in Chapter 2–*we're not the only ones involved here.* That's right. We need to think about how we're going to ensure that there is as much participation as possible on the part of the students and their parents. Yes, the administrators will want a role in this, too, but we will talk about how we can keep them happy in the next chapter.

Recording Assessments

Our Learning Assessment Plan tells us what we should be working toward (the learning outcomes) and how we intend to assess and monitor our students' growth toward achieving those outcomes. But how do we record our assessments and evaluations? With numbers? Letters? Descriptors? Narratives?

This is a critical philosophical point that we've reached. In view of the deference and adulation traditionally given to test scores, percentiles, and letter grades, we might be tempted to think in terms of similar types of numerical scales, such as marks out of 10 or a ranking from 1 to 5. Or we might consider supporting an alphabetical ranking such as *A* to *E*. Instead of numbers or letters, we might consider using words to signify the graduations, with *Excellent* at the top of the totem pole and *Hopeless* at the bottom.

Teachers who have used these systems to assess learning (or who are still encouraged or obliged to assess in these ways) will know the distortions and abuses such a system lends itself to. Lest I be accused of setting myself up as perfection itself, let me illustrate from my own past. When I first started teaching, our schools in New Zealand were required to rank all students on a 1 to 5 scale, 1 being "excellent," and 5 being "weak." We were also told to make our distribution of 1s to 5s conform to the "normal curve." The result of this was, when in doubt, give a student a 3, because it didn't matter so much if you had too many three's.

We distorted this "objective system" in other ways, too. We were required to assess our students twice a year. At the half-year assessment, there was an unwritten rule that said, "When in doubt, grade students down." So the potential 2s were given 3s, the possible 3s were given a 3-, and the 3- students were given a 4. This meant that at the end of the year, you could be generous and lift their grades. Suddenly the 4s became 3s, every 3- became a 3, and every 3 became a 2. The parents were always delighted. They would shake your hand and say you were a wonderful teacher and tell you how well their child had progressed in your class!

There were some other distortions, too. New Zealand teachers have to teach all subject areas of the curriculum, so we had to give assessments for, among other subjects, music and physical education. How did we do this? *"Hands up, all those children who practice a musical instrument at home!"* And those children were automatically ranked 1 or 2 in music. *"Hands up, all those who are members of a sports team or who go to the gym after school!"* They were automatically 1s or 2s in physical education!

The hard part was having to give students 5s. No matter how kind you tried to be, you knew it still hurt them. What tended to make it worse was the fact that the student with a 5 in one subject often scored a 5 in several subjects, and some were 5s in all subjects!

Now, we knew this was not very encouraging, so many schools used to give an additional assessment. We called this an "effort rating," and we gave it an alphabetical ranking of *A* to *E* so as not to confuse it with the numerical "attainment rating." An *A* meant that the students were working very hard and trying their best, and an *E* meant that they were just plain lazy. In our wisdom, we had decided that the effort rating didn't have to conform to the normal curve (There's nothing normal about effort!) so we were able to use this as a kind of soothing ointment to take the sting out of the 4s and 5s on the attainment rating.

We thought we were saying to the parents, "Look, your child isn't doing very well in mathematics (say). He's only a 5. But at least he tries really hard, so we've given him an *A* for effort." Of course, what we didn't realize was that this was really hitting the parents with a double whammy! The message they took from this was, in effect, "Not only is my child a 'dummy' in math, but he's working like crazy and he's *still* a dummy!"

To all these dubious practices, parents would add their own misconceptions and misinterpretations. For a start, they would count up how many 1s their child received so they could compare their child with someone else's. *"My child got three 1s." "Really? Mine got four! I think she's a genius!"* At the other end of the scale, children with too many 4s or 5s were left feeling that they were hopeless cases.

The basic problem was that these numerical and alphabetical ratings had no real meaning for parents other than a vague notion of success or approval. So it was no wonder these so-called measures of student learning really became something quite different: *measures of student worth!* Understandably, but sadly, to the parents, a 1 didn't just mean "very good learning"–it also meant "very good person." Conversely, a 5 didn't just mean "poor or unsatisfactory learning"–it was also interpreted as meaning that the student was a "poor and unsatisfactory person."

In time, teachers and members of the community came to recognize how inadequate and unhelpful this numerically graded information was. It didn't help the students because being told, for example, you were a 2 in math didn't tell you what you knew and could do or what you needed to work at next in order to continue your learning growth. The numbers didn't motivate you to learn, either. A 1 tended to tell you that you knew more than most people, so you could relax (though it didn't tell you more of *what*). A 3 said that you were just ordinary, so why bother. And a 5 told you that you were hopeless, so the best thing to do was to give up.

It didn't help the parents because they didn't know how to interpret these numbers, either. The single-scale numerical grading didn't tell them what their children knew and understood or what they were able or attitudinally empowered to do. They knew that a 4 or a 5 meant that something needed to be done, but the numbers didn't tell them what, so it just left them frustrated and upset–feelings they all too frequently, and of course unhelpfully, passed on to the students!

It didn't help the teachers because it didn't provide any specific information about the learning, other than how in summary it compared with the statistical construct of an "average child." It was not diagnostic–it didn't tell the teacher where the students needed help. It provided no help with planning because it didn't tell the teacher what the students knew, or where they needed assistance. It didn't help with "measuring" a student's learning growth, either, because it only provided a comparison with some semi-mythical "average."

So what did the teachers do?

Rather than trying to reduce a student's learning to mathematical summaries, they decided it was better to try to describe the student's learning as accurately and specifically as possible in words. As for trying to find a simple and valid measure of the student's learning progress, they decided it was far more helpful to compare what a child knows and can do now with what the same child knew and was able to do previously.

The result? The assessment became learning-specific, the classroom became learning-focused, and the teaching became learning-centered.

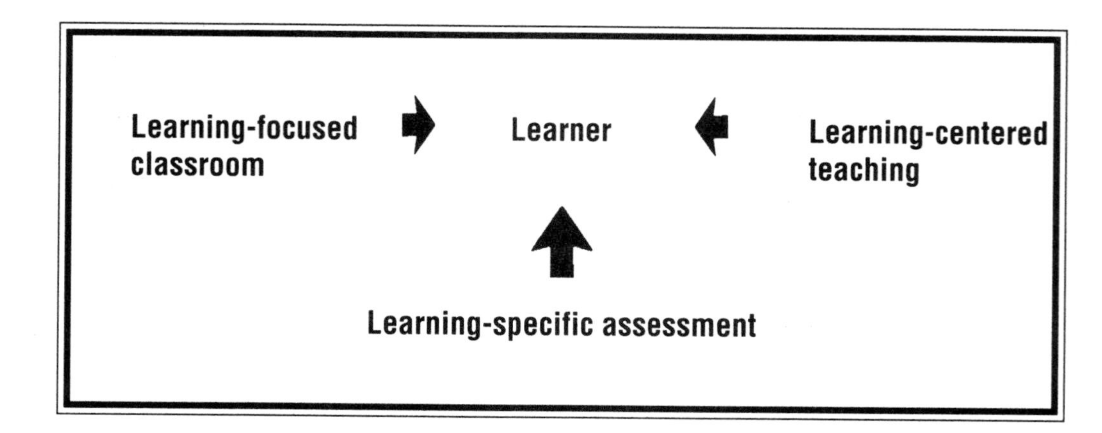

How Do We Describe the Learning Specifically?

This is easy–in our Learning Assessment Plan, we've already described what the learning outcomes should be. All we need now is some consistent way of describing the degree to which these outcomes have been met without straying back into the mine fields of grading scales. The following is a very simple approach that can be readily understood by everyone–teachers, students, parents, and school administrators.

The teacher takes each learning outcome and asks the following question.

As a result of observation, interaction, re-creation, reflection, simulation, or artifact collection, do I have evidence that this student:

(a) **knows this or is doing this or demonstrating this consistently (all the time), or**

(b) **is beginning to know or do or demonstrate this, or**

(c) **no, I don't have the evidence yet.**

We have to talk about knowing/doing/demonstrating because we framed our learning outcomes in terms of knowledges and understandings (knowing), skills and strategies (doing), and attitudes and values (demonstrating). But the answer should be a simple one: Yes, the student is doing this all the time, or is starting to do this, or is not yet doing it.

We are assessing:	**Knowledge and Understandings**	**Skills and Strategies**	**Attitudes and Values**
We ask:	Does the student know and fully understand this?	Is the student able to do this consistently?	Does the student demonstrate this consistently?
Or:	Is the student beginning to know and understand?	Is the student beginning to be able to do this?	Is the student beginning to demonstrate this?
Or:	Not yet?	Not yet?	Not yet?

How Do We Record the Learning for Each Student?

We simply add additional columns to our Learning Assessment Plan. Whenever the teacher completes an assessment for a student, the teacher reads the specific learning outcome and chooses which answer fits the evidence so far: *all the time, beginning to,* or *not yet.* If the answer is "all the time" (or if you prefer, "consistently"), then the teacher enters a 1 in this column and the date of the assessment in the next column. The reason for the number 1 is because later we will want to add these up to provide survey information, both for ourselves and for our school administrators. (We talk about this in Chapter 6.) We include the date so that we know at what point in the school year this learning outcome was mastered.

But if the answer is *beginning* to know or be able to do or demonstrate this, the teacher just enters the date of the assessment in the appropriate column. If the teacher wants to add any more information for the record, he or she writes the information, with the date, in the Other Comments column.

If the answer is *not yet,* then the teacher enters the date in the Not Yet column. A dated note regarding this entry can be included in the Other Comments column if the teacher wishes to do so.

The teacher can use the Other Comments column for a variety of purposes. It can be used to record specific observations or references to examples of work that illustrate the student's learning progress or current learning needs. The comments can also help document the teacher's assessments, by providing references to other teacher records, such as the teacher's anecdotal notebook. The entries in the Other Comments column can also include suggestions for instruction or planning, or questions about the learning that the teacher wishes to check out later.

Learning Assessment Record

Learning Area	Learning Outcome	Assessment Strategies	Assessment Tools	Is doing this all the time (Indicated by a "1")	Date of this Assessment (plus comments)	Is Beginning to do this (Indicated by dates of assessment checks and comments)	Not Yet (Indicated by dates of assessment and comments)	Other comments (with dates)
Language Arts *Reading*	**Skills and Strategies** *(Is able to . . .)*							
		Observation Interaction Artifact Collection	Anecdotal notebook Questioning (ask child to find information in a text) Teacher portfolio samples Student portfolio samples, also index to own portfolio	1	2/24: Observed using index for science project. Showed others. Listed in his "I Can Do" file, too.	2/10: Used index in own portfolio 2/18: Used index with astronomy project (with help).	1/17: Reading nonfiction in guided reading. Not able to locate information using an index.	1/17: Need to model index when discussing portfolios. Maybe class need? Check.

The Need for Regular Assessment Checks

The assessment process we are describing here is an accumulative one. In other words, we will be adding to the sum total of our knowledge and understanding of how our students are learning in a continuous way throughout the year. This is a liberating concept for teachers because it means we don't have to assess all students for the same learning at the same time. Wherever possible, assessment happens where and when learning happens.

However, with such an open-ended, accumulative, teacher-managed assessment process, it is important to have systems or prompts to make sure we really are doing regular and consistent learning assessment for individual students and the whole class.

The Learning Assessment Plan Time Line

One obvious way to ensure that we aren't leaving anyone out or neglecting any particular learning area is to go through the calendar for the year and nominate particular weeks as specific "assessment checkup" weeks.

However, it's important to add that this doesn't mean these are the only times when we are assessing and evaluating student learning! If we're going to make sure that assessment is an integral, or organic, part of learning, then it must be happening all the time. It's just that this is when we plan to give assessment more of our undivided attention. It's similar to going to the dentist: you might only go twice a year, but you still have to clean your teeth every day!

During some months you might plan to check all subjects, while during others you might want to focus on specific subject areas and give them the benefit of a little checking "halo."

It's important to have a general checkup early in the year in order to provide a base level against which to compare subsequent student learning growth throughout the year. Of course, you might end up with a lot of "not yets" on this first survey, simply because you haven't had time to see enough evidence to enter anything else. But that doesn't really matter. It simply means that you've made a start and drawn your first line in the sand–albeit a safe one!

The number of times you do a whole class survey and how often you visit a particular subject area for special attention will depend on the grade, your sstudents , and any other checking systems you might be using.

But your time line might start out looking something like this:

My Learning Assessment Plan Time Line

September Complete Assessment Audit Complete Learning Assessment Plan (but keep adding learning outcomes from ongoing planning) *Week 3: Check all subjects*	**February** *Week 4: Special assessment focus–Art, Music, and Physical Education*
October *Week 4: Assessment focus–Reading and Writing*	**March** *Week 4: Special assessment focus–Reading and Writing*
November *Week 2: Special assessment focus–Literature and Language Arts*	**April** *Week 4: Special assessment focus–Literature and Language Arts*
December *Week 2: Special assessment focus–Science and Social Studies*	**May** *Week 2: Special assessment focus–Science and Social Studies*
January Complete survey data for school administration *Week 4: Check all subjects*	**June** *Week 1: Check all subjects*

You might then go on to indicate when you think you will introduce specific assessment tools. Having done this, your time line might now begin to look more like the forms on the following pages.

My Learning Assessment Plan Time Line

September Do concepts about print test Begin Video Learning Log Take first photos Conduct Parent Survey Start anecdotal notebook Start running records in reading Start teacher's student portfolios Begin monthly reading audiotape *Week 3: Check all subjects*	**February** Continue Star of the Week Three-way conference (teacher/parent/student) Do goal setting Use anecdotal notebook regularly Continue with running records Continue building student portfolios Continue selecting work for documentation in teacher's student portfolios Monthly reading audiotape *Week 4: Special assessment focus–Art, Music, and Physical Education*
October Use anecdotal notebook regularly Start student portfolios Start reading logs Make and start Friday files Start running records in writing, too Start Think alouds in writing One-on-one conferences Peer portraits Do Mini time capsules Monthly reading audiotape *Week 4: Special assessment focus–Reading and Writing*	**March** Continue Star of the Week Use anecdotal notebook regularly Continue with running records Continue building student portfolios Continue selecting work for documentation in teacher's student portfolios Monthly reading audiotape *Week 4: Special assessment focus–Reading and Writing*
November Use anecdotal notebook regularly Continue with running records Continue building student portfolios Continue selecting work for documentation in teacher's student portfolios "How I am Doing" reflection for student portfolio Monthly reading audiotape Three-way conference (teacher/parent/student) Start Class Log *Week 2: Special assessment focus–Literature and Language Arts*	**April** Use anecdotal notebook regularly Continue with running records Continue building student portfolios Continue selecting work for documentation in teacher's student portfolios Monthly reading audiotape *Week 4: Special assessment focus–Literature and Language Arts*

December Use anecdotal notebook regularly Continue with running records Continue building student portfolios Student project reflections Monthly reading audiotape *Week 2: Special assessment focus–Science and Social Studies*	**May** Open mini time capsules Use anecdotal notebook regularly Continue with running records Continue building student portfolios Continue selecting work for documentation in teacher's student portfolios Monthly reading audiotape *Week 2: Special assessment focus–Science and Social Studies*
January Start Star of the Week Use anecdotal notebook regularly Continue with running records Continue building student portfolios Continue selecting work for documentation in teacher's student portfolios Monthly reading audiotape Complete survey data for school administration *Week 4: Check all subjects*	**June** Students complete own portfolios Complete teacher's student portfolios and cull material ready for transfer to next year's teacher Three-way conference (teacher/parent/student) Complete survey data for school administration *Week 1: Check all subjects*

Keeping Our Assessment Learner-Centered

Using the Learning Assessment Plan as a prompt to make sure all learning outcomes are considered–whether in "subject blocks" or in entirety–has its merits. But one thing to be wary of is becoming too preoccupied with the learning plan and, in so doing, losing sight of the learner. If we believe in the merits of a learner-centered classroom, then it is also important to consider learning holistically, student by student.

One way to help keep our learner-centered focus is to use the students themselves as a prompt. *Student Review Days* and *Star of the Week* are examples of this.

Student Review Days

In using this prompt, the teacher chooses a particular day of the week as the Student Review Day. In some school districts, Wednesdays are good days to set aside for this activity because there are generally fewer public holidays that fall on that day of the week. In addition, because it falls in the middle of the week, the class program will be a little more settled and predictable. Of course, the choice will also depend on the school and class programs.

The teacher goes through the calendar and, using the class attendance register or roll, enters two students' names alongside every Student Review Day. Once all of the students have had a review day, the teacher starts at the top of the roll again. It is a good idea to share this procedure with the students–in a positive way, of course! If they know their review day is coming up, they can help the teacher by having their work up-to-date and being ready to share their own reflections on their work.

On the review day, the teacher makes a special effort to observe the selected students throughout the day and to reflect on their learning. The teacher also conferences with the students and goes through all their current work. This provides an opportunity to talk about what they have learned, what they are in the process of learning , and what they need to learn. It's also a good opportunity to set some shared learning goals: the teacher helps the students define some achievable goals for themselves and then commits to helping the students achieve them. These are noted and are reconsidered on the next review day.

In addition to conferencing about current projects, the teacher observes the students throughout the day and writes anecdotal notes, as shown on the calendar on the next page.

Student Reviews for October

Sunday	Monday	Tuesday	Wednesday	Thursday	Friday	Saturday
1	2	3	4 Moira & Adam	5	6	7
8	9	10	11 Noona & Zak	12	13	14
15	16	17	18 Tina & Pablo	19	20	21
22	23	24	25 Quentin & Zelda	26	27	28
29	30	31				

Star of the Week

Another device that uses the students as the assessment reminder, or prompt, is the Star of the Week. The teacher chooses one child a week to be the weekly celebrity of the class. Let's say the child's name is Michael. Throughout the week, the teacher makes a point of giving Michael as much positive attention as possible, by choosing him for incidental tasks or special responsibilities, for example, or letting him have the pleasure of being able to choose other people for particular tasks, etc. The other students are also encouraged to "make sure Michael has a really great week!"

At the same time, the teacher makes a point of observing Michael in as many different situations as possible, not only in academic situations, but also in recreational and social settings.

The point of all this is to help the teacher really get to know the student. At the end of the week, the teacher makes a cardboard star–perhaps sprinkling glitter on it to make it a little more special–and conducts a "Star of the Week" presentation ceremony. Everyone sits in a circle, and the other students are encouraged to think of Michael's positive or praiseworthy qualities, using introductory phrases such as, "What I like about Michael is...," or, "What I think is special about Michael is..."

"What I liked about Michael this week was the way he helped me with some of my math problems. I understand how to do them now."

"What I like about Michael is his laugh. He laughs a lot and it makes me laugh."

"What I think is special about Michael is his drawings. He does some awesome drawings."

"What I liked about Michael this week was the story he wrote about visiting his grandmother. Maybe I'll write about my grandmother, too."

The teacher writes these statements, or a selection of them, on the star. The star is then officially presented to Michael, who takes it home to show his family. The next Monday, a new "Star of the Week" is chosen.

It is very easy for some children to be completely overlooked in a class. This device is helpful because it ensures that everyone in the class gets "fifteen minutes of fame." It also encourages the students to support one another and give one another encouragement and positive feedback. In addition, the Star of the Week helps prompt the teacher to give each child some intensive reflection and consideration.

Involving the Students in the Learning Assessment Process

So far, we have had a lot to say about what the *teacher* can do about assessment schedules and timing. But we aren't the only people on the assessment planet! For a start, there are the students. If one of the goals of education is to gradually empower our students to take increasing responsibility for their own learning, then as part of this process, they also need to take increasing responsibility for the assessment and evaluation of their own learning. Good learners are critical learners. They reflect on their learning in order to build on their strengths and shore up their weaknesses. They become increasingly self-monitoring and self-managing as learners.

But all this doesn't happen by accident, nor does it happen overnight. To help students achieve this self-monitoring/self-managing goal requires appropriate instruction, adequate but not overprotective "scaffolding," and positive, motivational support. To be effective assessors and evaluators of their own learning, students need to be able to use the same six assessment strategies their teachers use.

For starters, they need to be encouraged to make observations about their own learning and to value their own observations. To do this, students can use the same assessment tools their teachers use. The student's Personal Journal, for example, is an excellent place for children to note their own observations about their learning. They can keep their own "I can do" lists or "My future challenges" lists (based on their observations), or "All about me" and autobiographies. They can complete their own post-its or mailing label observations for the teacher/student anecdotal record, and they can contribute their own observations about their learning in student/teacher conferences, peer or group conferences, and three-way conferences.

Encouraging students to work collaboratively also hones the interactive skills they need in order to assess their own learning. Activities like Chat Checks, Buzz Groups, and Talking Stick give students supportive situations for testing themselves and finding out who they are, what they can do, and what they feel and believe about themselves and their learning. "Dear Author" and Today's Heroes are activities that allow students to interact positively in writing.

"Dear Author"

Main assessment strategy: Interaction

When students publish a book in the classroom, they add some extra pages at the end of the book. These are arranged in blocks and each is headed "Dear Author." When other students read the book, they are encouraged to "write to the author" by entering a comment or question in this section. Readers write in alternating boxes. The space between the boxes is left blank in case the author wants to write a comment in reply to a reader.

Dear Author, I really enjoyed your story, Brad; especially the part where your canoe capsized. Toni
I enjoyed writing that part, too. Brad
Wow, Brad! Lucky to be alive! Did this really happen to you? Shirley
Yes, it really did. We were really scared, too. Brad
Were you wearing life jackets? Scott
Dad won't let us take the canoe out unless we have them on. It was just as well, wasn't it? Brad
The best bit for me was the way you say what was buzzing in your head afterward. Vinnie

Today's heroes

Main assessment strategy: Interaction
Additional strategy: Observation

Using this activity, the teacher prepares some "Today's Heroes" nomination forms and explains that they are for anyone who notices someone else doing some very good work or something that is really clever or helpful to other people. These nomination forms are then posted on a special bulletin board with the heading "Today's Heroes." At the end of the day, the teacher reads aloud the comments and the students applaud the new class "heroes."

Nomination Form for Today's Heroes

I wish to nominate *Vince* to become one of *Today's Heroes!* because ...
he has painted a wonderful frog for our nature table. It looks just right. We especially like the eyes.

Nominator: *Craig*

The ***re-creative*** models we provide in the classroom, such as *retelling, redrawing, dramatization,* and *rewriting,* help students internalize ways of appraising their own learning experiences.

The more we encourage them to be *reflective,* the better equipped they will be to monitor and manage their own learning. *Goal setting,* "All About Me," personal journals, and other pieces of reflective writing provide students with opportunities to participate in the assessment and evaluation of their own work.

The Learning Detective is another useful activity for helping students reflect on their learning. The teacher provides the students with some forms like the ones on the following page.

The Learning Detective
Case Notes

I have voted that ______________ (the suspect's name) knows all about:

or is able to:

Evidence:

Signed
Me! (____________________)

A completed Learning Detective form might look like this:

The Learning Detective
Case Notes

I have voted that ___*Jody*___ (the suspect's name) knows all about:

or is able to:
Use the spelling checker on the computer.

Evidence:
She has been showing Micah and Toby how to use it. And the teacher.

Signed
Me! (___*Jody*___)

Viewpoint frames are useful reflective devices, too. The students are encouraged to reflect from a particular person's viewpoint. They are encouraged to reflect on their writing with the following example.

Viewpoints	
One thing my teacher will like about this piece is:	One thing my friends will like about this piece is:
One thing my parents will like about this piece is:	One thing I like about this piece is:

Students can even use self-testing and other ***simulated*** learning experiences to learn more about their own unique skills and strengths.

To show I know all about electricity, can I write down 10 things about it?

> Dear Mom,
>
> To show I am a good speller, please choose 10 words from anywhere in my stories or my science project and ask me to spell them for you.
>
> Your spellerific offspring,
>
> Claude

They might also draw immense pleasure and gain helpful insight from the learning artifacts they collect and store in their own personal student portfolios. The processes of selection, organization, presentation, and documentation ("Why I Chose this Piece," etc.) are all valuable self-appraisal activities. But perhaps the most powerful feature of the student portfolio is the impact it can have on student attitudes and values. When students proudly share their portfolios with their friends and family, they are learning to celebrate their own achievements and value their own feelings and beliefs.

We can summarize these as follows:

Some activities to involve our students in the assessment process

Observation	Interaction	Re-creation	Reflection	Simulation	Artifact Collection
Personal Journals	Conferences	Retellings	Goal setting	Self-tests	Student's portfolio
"I can do" lists	Buzz groups	Redrawings	"Star of the Day"		
"My Future Challenges"	Chat Checks	Dramatization	Student Review		
"All About Me"	Talking Stick	Rewritings	Class log		
Video log	Dear Author...				
	Friday Folders				

Involving the Parents in the Learning Assessment Process

Traditionally teachers have talked about "reporting to parents." The phrase itself is revealing! It implies a one-way process that is initiated by the teacher, with little or no opportunity for input or feedback on the part of the parents. This was reinforced by the way the reporting was done: usually the teacher provided the parents with a written report on the student's progress. The report was sent home and the parents then came to school to react or comment on the teacher's report. As for the student's involvement in all this–the whole business was strictly for "grown-ups."

Teachers are now challenging this view–in part because they recognize that the traditional approach was unfair to parents, but also because it was just plain silly. Parents can contribute invaluable information on their children's health history, interests, enthusiasms, hobbies, temperament, relationships with friends, relationships within the family, life experiences, moods, and morale. In other words, they can "fill in the picture."

They can also provide feedback on the learning by telling teachers what they see as the impact of what happens at school on what the child does at home. Parents and students can work collaboratively with the teacher to contribute to the assessment process, and they can follow up and help implement decisions arrived at two-way (parent/teacher) and three-way (parent/student/teacher) conferences. We'll discuss reporting to parents more specifically in the next chapter. But in the meantime, it is useful to review some ideas for helping parents to participate in the assessment process.

Making contact

If we want parents to participate in the learning assessment process, it's essential that they get to hear about it! One simple way of achieving this is to send home a letter at the start of the year with some information about the learning you have planned, along with some suggestions on how the parents can help. Your letter might look something like the one on the following page.

Madison School
Wide Forest Valley

Dear Parent,

I want to share with you a little advance "publicity" for some of the exciting things we're going to be doing this year. The third and fourth grade teachers have been working together and sharing ideas, and we've come up with some great theme topics for some of our major content studies this year. The plan is as follows:

September:	December:	March:
October:	January:	April:
November:	February:	May:

Please take every opportunity to let you child tell you all about the current theme topics. Once the year is under way, we're going to start "Friday Folders." During the week, the children will be choosing some of the special things they've been doing and placing the work in these plastic folders. They will bring these home most Fridays to show you. Ask them to tell you all about the work and why they chose to bring those pieces home.

They will also bring home a "Friday Folder Response" form. If you have time, please write a positive comment or two on the form. I'd be delighted, and, of course, so would your child.

The Friday Folder needs to be returned to school at the start of the next week, so please make sure it goes into your child's backpack or book bag before he or she leaves home on Monday morning.

The children have begun their own portfolios, and by the end of the year those portfolios will be bulging with all kinds of interesting things to show how much they have learned. The children are already looking forward to being able to share these with you and tell you all about what they're doing as a class on parent night.

We will be having three-way conferences later in the year. I hope to meet with you and your child, and together we'll talk about how everything is going and see if we can all help your child do even better. I'll be writing to tell you all about those conferences shortly before they're held.

I've enclosed a form headed, "Things I'd Like the Teacher to Know About My Child." Please fill it out and have your child return it to school as soon as possible. This will help me get to know your child.

If there is anything of a confidential nature that you would like to share with me, please call the school office to arrange a meeting, or specify a suitable time when I can contact you. If you have a computer, you can always send me a confidential e-mail. My e-mail address is: Teach@schoolhouse.com.

In the meantime, I look forward to your comments. I'm sure we're all going to have a great year in room 7.

Yours truly,

(Teacher's name)

Electronic connections

If you are using computers, why not prepare a database with parents' names and addresses so you can use a "mail merge" function to personalize these letters to parents. Or better still, let your students prepare the database!

And while we're on the subject of computers, if your school has its own web page, why not put this kind of information there, too, so parents who are on-line can read it at home?

Friday Folders response sheet

The Friday Folders response sheet might look like this:

Friday Folders

Dear Family,

Here is my Friday Folder for Friday, ________________.

I have included three things:

1.

I chose this because:

2.

I chose this because:

3.

I chose this because:

Please write two positive comments on my Friday Folder for this week:

Thanks,

____

Positive comments:

1. The special thing I liked…

2. Also…

Signed: __________________________

A completed Friday Folders response sheet might look like this

Friday Folders

Dear Family,

Here is my Friday Folder for Friday, *October 27*.

I have included three things:

1. *A story I wrote about runny cheese*

I chose this because: *it was funny, and anyway, you know what I did with the pizza last week!*

2. *My math puzzle*

I chose this because: *Janine and I had a lot of trouble getting it to work, and now it does. See if you can work it out.*

3. *My painting of leaves*

I chose this because: *I like it, and Janine said she did, too.*

Please write two positive comments on my Friday Folder for this week:

Thanks,

Lesley

Positive comments:

1. The special thing I liked...*your story about the stretchy cheese. It happened just like you said. And you're right. It was funny!*

2. Also...*those leaves! They are beautiful. They made me think about fall, when they all come tumbling down.*

Signed: *Marie Klister*

Things I'd like the teacher to know about my child

The "Things I'd Like the Teacher to Know about My Child" form might look something like this:

Madison School
Wide Forest Valley

Things I'd Like the Teacher to Know about My Child

These are three things ______________ is good at:

1.

2.

3.

If I had to choose six things I really want for __________, they would be:

1. I want my child to know and understand

2.

3. I want my child to be able to

4.

5. I want my child to be or feel

6.

Do I have any worries or concerns at this stage?
No _____
Yes _____

Please contact the office and make an appointment to see me if you have any worries or concerns you want to discuss.

Thank you for sharing this information with me. It will help me to help your child.

What did you do at school today?

So often when children come home from school their parents inevitably ask them something like, "So, what happened at school today?" And almost as predictably, the reply goes something like, "Oh... nothing." This is a pity, because one of the best ways to communicate with parents and enlist their help in the task of developing the child's learning is to work through the child.

Part of the problem is that parents and children don't always know how to begin a dialog about school. Questions like, "What did you do at school today?" or, "How was school?" or even, "Did you have a good day at school today?"–no matter how well-intentioned–are just too nebulous and vague. One way to help parents get into a dialog with their children is to get the students to make up and write a good riddle-like question. They then take this question home and give it to their parents. Of course, it doesn't have to be answered the moment they are in the door. The parents might like to set aside a special time, such as over dinner, for having this dialog about school.

The riddle in a note might look something like this:

February 7

Dear Mom,

Here is one good question you can ask me about what we did in school today:

What is red and goes fast and makes a lot of noise as it travels down the street?

Love,

Micah

The "Great Home Bulletin Board Competition"

This is another enjoyable way to help parents participate in their child's learning. A teacher wrote the letter on the next page with the students as a shared writing activity. Copies were then run off for each child to take home. The teacher provided pieces of cardboard for the students to make their own bulletin boards. They had to measure the space where the board was to be placed at home and then cut the cardboard to fit (good practical math!). Then they painted a border and prepared the heading. Plastic sleeves for examples of work were attached.

Children who didn't have a suitable wall space at home (or whose parents didn't want them putting anything on the wall) used an old carton as a freestanding bulletin board. They covered the carton with paper, painted it, and then attached the transparent plastic sleeves.

The Great Home Bulletin Board Competition

Dear Parents,

What do you do with all those exciting bits and pieces we kids bring home from school? Maybe you attach them to the refrigerator door with magnets. Or maybe you pin them up on the wall. Or maybe you leave them on the kitchen table for everyone else to look at and spill their coffee on. Or maybe you just hang them from a string in the garage.

Why not get your child (that's me!) to help make a bulletin board for these things? We've been talking about this in class, so I already have some great ideas. Maybe it could go in my bedroom. Or maybe it could go in the kitchen. Or maybe *you* have a great idea.

Anyway, we're going to have a competition, and we'd like you to help. All you have to do is help me find somewhere to put this bulletin board. We'll make it at school and it will be my job to keep changing the things that are displayed on it.

Also, each week I have to write two good questions or two interesting sentences to go on the bulletin board.

Our teacher is going to buy a disposable camera, and we're going to take it in turns to bring it home and photograph our home bulletin boards. We have to be in the picture, so I'll need someone to take the photo for me.

When we've all had a turn, the teacher will have the film developed, and we'll have a display of our bulletin boards in our classroom.

That's the prize–to have a photo of your bulletin board on our class bulletin board! Yep, this is one competition where everyone gets to win!

Yours newsworthily,

Zelda

Class video log response form

Keeping a class video log is another great way to document the learning in the classroom. (See pages 61-62 for ideas on how to go about creating this video log.) But this is also an opportunity for parents and students to share in the learning assessment. Have your students prepare a Video Response Form so that parents have an opportunity to interact and also give feedback. In the example below, the students had to sign for the video when they were borrowing it to make sure it didn't get lost. (This teacher always kept a copy of the video, in case the worst happened!) The students also had to write two questions for their parents. For this class, the teacher required the students to actually write their parents' answers. There were two reasons for this. First, the teacher knew that some of the parents were not very confident about writing in English, and he didn't want them to feel threatened or humiliated by the exercise. But more importantly, it was an opportunity for the parents and the children to interact and work together on a school task.

Madison School
Wide Forest Valley
Video Response Form

Dear Parents,

Our class has been making a video, showing us at work. We videotape the class for two minutes every week at the same time and from the same angle. We are allowed to borrow the video in order to show our parents. After we have watched the video, I have to ask you two questions. My questions are:

1. *What am I looking at with the magnifying glass on October 24th?*
   Answer (I have to write it):

2. *Do you like our class papier-mache' puppets on January 19th?*
   Answer (I have to write it):

Thank you,

Davida

The class log

The class log is an excellent idea for helping students remember what has happened during the school day. As a result, it "primes" them for a full discussion and review of the day when they get home.

Chapter Review: The "All the World's a Classroom" Test

All the World's a Classroom

Part A

Answer **Yes, No,** or **Heck! I don't know!** to the following questions.

Do your students learn anything by talking and interacting with their parents?

Yes ❑ No ❑ Heck! I don't know! ❑

Do your students learn anything by talking and interacting with the other members of their families?

Yes ❑ No ❑ Heck! I don't know! ❑

Do your students learn anything by talking with their friends?

Yes ❑ No ❑ Heck! I don't know! ❑

Do your students learn anything from the TV programs they watch?

Yes ❑ No ❑ Heck! I don't know! ❑

Do your students learn anything from the books and magazines they read?

Yes ❑ No ❑ Heck! I don't know! ❑

Do your students learn anything from computers and computer games?

Yes ❑ No ❑ Heck! I don't know! ❑

Do your students learn anything by playing with toys and games in their homes?

Yes ❑ No ❑ Heck! I don't know! ❑

Do your students learn anything by listening to other people?

Yes ❑ No ❑ Heck! I don't know! ❑

Do your students learn anything from the models of behavior provided by the people around them?

Yes ❑ No ❑ Heck! I don't know! ❑

Do your students learn anything from the ads they hear or see?

Yes ❑ No ❑ Heck! I don't know! ❑

All the World's a Classroom

Do your students learn anything from the music they listen to?

Yes ❑ No ❑ Heck! I don't know! ❑

Do your students learn anything from their personal heroes?

Yes ❑ No ❑ Heck! I don't know! ❑

Do your students learn anything by daydreaming?

Yes ❑ No ❑ Heck! I don't know! ❑

Do your students learn anything by thinking about the things they already know?

Yes ❑ No ❑ Heck! I don't know! ❑

Part B

Answer **A lot! A little**, or **Not much, I guess** to the following questions.

What part do all the things that are happening outside the classroom play in what your students are learning inside the classroom?

A lot ❑ A little ❑ Not much, I guess ❑

Part C

(And this is the real toughie!) So, what are the implications for assessment and evaluation of learning?

____

____

____

____

____

Chapter 6

Getting Results

Using the Learning Assessment Record to Meet School and District Needs

In This Chapter

- **Assessment for Instruction versus Assessment for Accountability**
- **Using the Learning Assessment Record to Survey School and Grade Achievement**
- **Surveying Subject Area Learning Progress**
- **Class Learning Progress Profiles**
- **Other Uses for Assessment Surveys**
- **The Learning Assessment Record and Traditional Report Cards**
- **The Seven Habits of Highly Successful Teacher/Parent Communicators**
- **How to Improve the Traditional Report Card**
- **Electronic Report Cards**
- **The Three-Way Conference**
- **Chapter Review: The Teacher Personality Type Test**

Assessment for Instruction versus Assessment for Accountability

Way back in Chapter 1, we declared that one of the major challenges facing educators today is reconciling the need teachers have for assessment to support the learning with the need administrators and the community at large have for assessment to establish accountability.

So far, we've concentrated on dealing with the former. This is, in part, because we believe the need to facilitate learning is more important than accountability checking–it's pointless to check the learning if you haven't *got* any learning! But also because, contrary to popular belief, we don't think the two need to be seen as incompatible.

It is true that administrators and teachers do not have the same assessment needs. They focus on different areas, and they're doing different things with the assessment data. We can summarize this as follows:

Teachers	Administrators
Assessment focus: Individual learning growth.	Assessment focus: Group performance by grade level and/or age level.
Assessment needed for monitoring of individual and small-group learning and to assist with the planning and fine-tuning of the instruction.	Assessment needed for judging the curriculum and learning materials, the allocation of funds, the school system, and the effectiveness of the teaching.
Need continuous and ongoing individual assessment.	Need "snapshot" surveys at regular intervals.
Need a lot of detail to document the complexity and uniqueness of individual learning.	Need group trends and summaries, not individual documentation. Too much detail is confusing and makes it hard to see the forest for the trees.
Answerable to students, parents, and school administrators.	Answerable to parents, school district administrators, the community, politicians, and the media.

Even though the administrator's assessment needs might differ from those of the classroom teacher, it doesn't necessarily follow that all these needs can't be met in a single, unified way. Traditionally, teachers and administrators have had trouble reconciling their procedures because of their varying mind-sets with regard to assessment, and because of the assessment practices that stem from those mind-sets.

The following diagram summarizes some of the key differences between the traditional approach to assessment and the process we have been describing in this book.

Traditional approaches to assessment	Assessment process described in this book
The traditional idea was that you assessed learning by means of one approach–the test–preferably a standardized test.	Learning is assessed by six major strategies and a wide range of assessment tools.
The tests usually were administered in a group situation.	The assessment is done largely on an individual basis.
The tests were administered and evaluated by the teachers.	The teachers share assessment responsibility with students and parents.
The tests weren't based directly on the learning, but instead sampled knowledge and understanding and simulated experiences to test the students' skills and strategies.	The assessment is derived directly from the learning and is, as much as possible, an integral, or organic, part of the learning.
The aim was to provide a snapshot survey of learning at one time; therefore, everyone had to take the tests at the same time.	The aim is to monitor learning on a continuous basis; therefore, assessment goes on all the time. However, snapshot surveys of student groups or content areas are also possible at any time. (This is what this chapter is all about.)

Traditional approaches to assessment	Assessment process described in this book
Students couldn't do anything else while they were taking the tests. For example, they couldn't complete the tests in the midst of a learning experience because that might prejudice the reliability of the tests. As a result, assessment and learning were kept separate.	Assessment is seen as supporting and enhancing the learning, so it is important that assessment and learning are *not* separated.
Because everyone had to do the tests at the same time, factors such as fluctuation in student health, attendance, motivation, and morale could introduce irregularities into the snapshot results.	Because assessment is continuous and cumulative, variations in performance (e.g., children absent or in poor health) will not contaminate the assessment information. Snapshot surveys are derived from accumulated evidence up to the day of the survey, not just from assessment data gathered on a particular day.
The results were evaluated by comparing them with a standardized "norm"–a statistical construct that was usually validated by comparing the test results with other test result "norms."	The assessment data is not evaluated by comparison with statistical norms of standardized tests, but rather against what the students are supposed to learn (the learning outcomes in the Learning Assessment Plan) and their own previous learning.
The results were expressed in abstract numerical terms that required sophisticated knowledge to interpret; therefore, they meant little to the student or parent and had little diagnostic value for the classroom teacher.	The results are expressed in language that specifically describes the learning–language the teacher, student, and parent can understand and use.
Teachers evaluated group learning and extrapolated individual learning needs from the group data.	Teachers evaluate individual learning and combine these to arrive at group learning data.

The main task of this chapter is to show how the assessment process we have been describing here will meet the needs of both the teacher and the administrator.

Using the Learning Assessment Record to Survey School and Grade Achievement

What do administrators need in the way of assessment data in order to meet accountability requirements? Primarily, they need regular snapshot surveys, validated with evidence, to show in summary or broad terms where the learning is in

- each grade or class;
- and in each subject area in each grade or class;
- and, for accountability purposes, they need to be able to make comparisons between where the learning is now and where the learning was previously (i.e., to demonstrate and measure in broad terms how learning is progressing).

Administrators need this assessment to be done regularly at specific times of the year. The number of snapshots and when they are taken will vary from school district to school district. Some districts will want to do this kind of snapshot survey at least twice a year–common policy calls for these snapshots at the halfway point and at again at the end of the year. Other districts might want to do three snapshot surveys–a preliminary one at the start of the year to provide a baseline for the survey, one at the midpoint, and a third at the end of the year. This is a matter administrators themselves might want to decide, though a little discussion with the teachers can be valuable (He says gently!) and a little collaborative decision-making wouldn't hurt.

But once the snapshot surveys become a regular occurrence, information becomes cumulative and administrators are able to follow each cohort of students through the school and see trends and patterns and make medium and long-term plans with much greater confidence and surety.

So, how do we use the Learning Assessment Record to meet the administrator's needs?

Throughout the year, the teacher has been assessing the learning according to the learning outcomes criteria. For each learning outcome, the teacher evaluates the evidence and records whether the student is demonstrating the learning consistently, beginning to demonstrate it, or not yet demonstrating it.

When a student clearly demonstrates a learning outcome consistently, the teacher enters a 1 in that column in the Learning Assessment Record (see extract below).

Extract from a Learning Assessment Record

Learning Outcomes	**Is Doing This All the Time (Indicated by a 1)**	**Date of this assessment**	**Is Beginning to do This (Indicated by dates of assessment checks)**	**Not Yet (Indicated by dates of assessment checks)**	**Other Comments (With dates)**
Language Arts Reading					
Skills and Strategies *(Is able to...)*					
Use an index to locate information	1	3/24/99	10/4/98 1/18/99	7/4/98	10/4/98: used index in own portifolio 1/18/99: used index with astronomy project (with help) 3/24/98: observed using index for science project. Showed others. Listed in his "I can do" file, too.

It is this data that we can use to meet the needs of our school administrators. On the chosen assessment survey day, the teacher converts this data from the Learning Assessment Record into a snapshot survey in three simple steps.

Step 1

The teacher adds up all the 1s scored by the students. For example, let's say the total for our class is 480.

> This process is even easier if the Learning Assessment Record is stored on a computer. If you're working in Microsoft Word for Windows, for example, all you have to do is store all students' work in one continuous table, repeating the learning outcomes for each student. To add up the 1s, just number the rows and then choose "formula" from the "table" menu and instruct the computer to add all the numbers in that particular column, from row 1 to the last row above the total.

Step 2

Keep in mind that the total number of learning outcomes to be assessed will probably be different from grade to grade, so this raw score is now converted into a percentage of the total number of learning outcomes for the grade range, as follows.

Formula:

$$\frac{\text{Number of 1s for all learning outcomes for all students in the class.}}{\text{Total possible number of learning outcomes (i.e., total number of learning outcomes being assessed for the grade range) multiplied by the number of students in the class (20).}} \times \frac{100}{1} = \%$$

(grade's percentage of the learning outcomes)

Example:

$$\frac{480}{84 \times 20} \times \frac{100}{1} = 28.57\%$$

Step 3

The result is the grade's percentage of the learning outcomes attained at this point in time. But this figure doesn't tell us enough.

Since we are assessing learning in multiple grade ranges rather than in single grades, one would expect the percentage of completed learning outcomes to be greater in those classes at the upper end of the range. So, what we need to do is work out the difference between the previous percentage of learning outcomes and the current percentage of learning outcomes.

However, this figure can vary according to how much time has elapsed between the two surveys. So we now divide the difference between the two survey percentages by the number of months that have elapsed between them. As a result, we have a measure of the learning progress expressed in percentage points per month.

Formula:

Current grade percentage minus previous grade percentage divided by the number of months between snapshot surveys	=	Number of percentage points of learning progress per month.

Example:

$$\frac{28.57 - 19.07}{6} = 1.58$$

= 1.58 percentage points of learning progress
= the General Learning Progress Survey

We call these percentage points of learning progress ***General Learning Progress Surveys***, so as not to confuse them with the more precise and detailed individual assessment information in the teacher's learning assessment record, anecdotal records, and student and teacher portfolios.

Surveying Subject Area Learning Progress

We can use a similar process to arrive at assessment summaries for specific subject areas. For example, if we are seeking to do an assessment summary for mathematics for a particular grade or class, we use the same three steps.

1. We add up all the 1s scored by the students in the mathematics area.

> ***Example:***
>
> 210 1s

2. We then convert this to a percentage of the total number of learning outcomes for mathematics.

> ***Example:***
>
> $$\frac{210}{32 \times 20} \times \frac{100}{1} = 32.81\%$$

3. We then subtract the previous grade percentage for mathematics from the current percentage grade and divide the result by the number of months between snapshot surveys. The result is the grade or class' assessment survey expressed in percentage points of learning progress per month.

> ***Example continued:***
>
> $$\frac{32.81 - 27.4}{6}$$
>
> = .9 percentage points per month of learning progress
>
> = **the mathematics learning progress survey**

Class Learning Progress Profiles

We can use a similar process to provide a class profile for the learning progress in a particular subject or for all subjects.

1. We add up all the 1s for each learning outcome for the whole class. (It's possible to have the computer do this operation for us.)
2. The results are then totaled on a blank copy of the Learning Assessment Record.
3. The teacher checks the profile, looking especially at the high and low totals in order to see if there are particular areas that need special consideration when planning the instruction.

Other Uses for Assessment Surveys

- The classroom teacher is also able to analyze the learning outcomes within a subject area in order to see patterns (learning outcomes with lower scores versus learning outcomes with high scores) and plan subsequent instruction.

- The teacher can also do a General Learning Survey for each child in order to get some idea of how each student is progressing across all subjects. This is helpful in that it might alert the teacher to students who need particular attention, but we should use this information with caution. The danger is that the teacher can become infatuated with the numbers and loose sight of the child and the specific learning details.

- We can make broad comparisons within the school. For example, we can say the learning in Class A has gained four percentage points per month over the last six months, while over the same period of time, the learning in Class B has increased by only three percentage points per month.

- We can make comparisons between different subject areas for an age range of a grade range. We can say, for example, the assessment summaries for science are much lower than for all the other subject areas for grades 3 to 6, so maybe that is an area we need to focus on for some professional development.

Of course, what this assessment does not do is show us *why* there is a difference. That is where assessment moves into evaluation, which requires the participation of the teachers involved.

- The survey data can help us when we're making decisions about special funding, the purchase of resource materials, or the placement of personnel. For example, if the survey data indicates an area of the school where the learning progress seems to be significantly slower, the administrator might decide to purchase more books or resource materials for that area, organize consultants to assist with professional development for the teachers, provide additional staffing, or regroup the students into smaller classes.

- If the assessment records are passed on at the end of the year from teacher to teacher so that information is allowed to accumulate, then we can follow an age cohort or a group of students through their schooling and chart trends over an extended time frame. As a result, for example, changes in teaching methodology and teaching resources can be assessed over long-term periods, thus giving valuable feedback on school systems and funding decisions. This also provides a kind of internal auditing of assessment standards because teachers won't be tempted to "inflate" their evaluations since they know they will be "checked" by subsequent teachers.

- We can use these General Learning Progress Surveys to prepare graphs of student learning. Such visual representations often help us get a clearer picture of our students' learning strengths and needs and enable us to plan the instruction more effectively. This kind of presentation can be very helpful for parents and the community, too.

- If necessary, we can make some broad comparisons between schools, too. One of the major weaknesses of traditional comparisons between schools based on test scores is that schools drawing on students from more affluent areas would inevitably find it easier to maintain higher grade scores than schools drawing on less advantaged students, simply because their students tended to start at a higher and more consistent level. This in turn tended to perpetuate and even exacerbate the situation, because the more affluent parents were generally in a better position to make a choice of schools and so would tend to choose those with the higher test scores. Teachers were attracted to these schools, too, and as a result, administrators could choose from a larger pool of teaching talent. So better teachers meant even better test scores!

- Administrators can also use this data as preliminary material for evaluating teacher effectiveness. Preliminary, because the survey data gives only a very broad summary, and one that is based on learning "peaks." To continue the metaphor, it doesn't give us a detailed topography of the whole learning terrain between those peaks. However, the survey data will be sufficient to sound appropriate alarm bells and encourage administrators to look more closely at the teachers' practice. When trying to assess teacher effectiveness in more depth, one would expect administrators to utilize the full range of assessment strategies we have discussed in this book for use with students: observation, interaction, re-creation, reflection, simulation, and artifact collection.

Traditional systems tended to rely on evidence of *attainment*, which was usually derived from simulated assessment strategies such as standardized tests. What was lacking was some means of indicating authentic learning *progress*. Some teachers working with disadvantaged students might have been fostering extraordinary learning, but the test scores and grade levels didn't reflect that learning. On the other hand, teachers working with advantaged students might have been able to coast along and still not worry because they were being judged by their students' attainment level, not their learning progress. The assessment process we have been describing here can provide evidence of *attainment*–because we can accurately, and with documentation, describe what they have learned to date–and evidence of learning *progress*–because we can describe and document their learning over time.

When considering this process for matters of school and teacher effectiveness, it is important to keep in mind the fact that these statistics give a very broad and inevitably far from precise picture. However, they do have one great virtue: they are grounded in documented evidence of authentic learning. As such, they are a much fairer, a more honest, and a more transparent measure of school and teacher effectiveness than student grade-point averages and standardized test scores.

The Learning Assessment Record and Traditional Report Cards

Sending home report cards was the traditional way in which teachers related results to parents. Parents read the report cards to "check their child's grades." They wanted to know if their child's grades were "up or down" when compared with the last report card. The student's work was traditionally reported in some form of number or letter code. Parents often counted up the number or letter grades to see whether or not it was a "good report."

But number and letter grades tell parents very little about what their children actually know and understand or what they are able and attitudinally empowered to do. All parents gather from these is a vague sense that their child's learning is "going well," "going OK," or "not going very well at all." That's not only meager information, it's decidedly unhelpful. All parents were able to do about the traditional report card was applaud the grades, or accept them, or express disappointment or concern about them.

We think we as teachers can do a lot better than that. For a start, we can spell out some principles we ought to be applying when reporting to parents. How about *The Seven Habits of Highly Successful Teacher/Parent Communicators?*

The Seven Habits of Highly Successful Teacher/Parent Communicators

1. **We should respect the parents' intelligence, feelings, and rights as parents.**
   In other words, we should communicate accurately and fairly in language parents can understand. We also need to be sensitive, but that doesn't mean we fudge results or hide behind jargon and teacher-speak. We should be as specific as possible, avoiding vague, meaningless phrases like "progressing well" and "could try harder." And we shouldn't use number and letter codes that are liable to be meaningless, misunderstood, or misinterpreted.

2. **We should provide a context for the learning we are describing.**
   In other words, we should illustrate our points with anecdotal evidence and examples from the students' portfolios, etc.

3. **We should emphasize the positive. We should tell parents what their children now know and understand, what they can do, and what empowering attitudes and values they bring to the learning.**
   This also means we should avoid the undermining of positive comments by adding negative tags: "*Michael wrote some wonderful poems in his Sky Anthology, but he needs to work harder at punctuation and presentation.*"

4. **We should depict learning progress by providing comparisons with previous learning.**
   This means, instead of encouraging their children to be "better than the other children," we help parents to encourage their children to strive to achieve their personal best. Ironically, for many students, achieving their personal best might in fact be harder than being better than everyone else!

5. **We should always have the highest expectations possible for our students.**
   Low expectations become self-fulfilling prophecies. This also means we should be highly suspicious of all labels (ADD, etc.), because they focus attention on what students *can't* do rather than what they *can* do and cause us to lower our expectations.

6. **We should empower parents to participate and collaborate.**
   This doesn't mean we give up our responsibilities as "learning professionals," but it *does* mean we inform parents, we are honest with parents, we listen to parents, and we try to involve them in the excitement of their children's learning adventures.

7. **We should foster three-way communication–between teacher, student, and parent.**

How to Improve the Traditional Report Card

For a start, we can directly relate the report card to the student learning by basing it on the Learning Assessment Record. A simple but highly specific report card can be devised by selecting some key learning outcomes for each subject area for the class. We need to make a selection because the number of learning outcomes is probably going to be too unwieldy to be reproduced on a conventional report card. As part of this selection, care should be taken to ensure that there is adequate representation for all three aspects of learning: knowledge and understandings, skills and strategies, and attitudes and values. A few additional lines can be included for each subject area so the teacher can include significant learning outcomes the student has mastered that are not listed on the report card.

Alongside each learning outcome are three columns headed "Is doing this all the time," "Is beginning to do this," "Not seen yet" (or words to that effect), and a wider column headed "Comments." To complete the report card, the teacher checks the appropriate column for each learning outcome and, wherever helpful, writes an appropriate note in the Comments column.

There should also be space on the report card for more open-ended narrative teacher comments.

The sample report card on the following pages illustrates these points.

Social and Collaborative skills

	Almost Always	Some of the time	Not yet
Shows self-confidence		√	
Respects others		√	
Contributes and participates in group activities		√	

Comments:
Jody is always helpful in the class. Her confidence is growing and she is now less shy about sharing in small group situations.

Self-Management Skills

	Almost Always	Some of the time	Not yet
Makes decisions for self			√
Shows initiative			√
Takes responsibility for own possessions and materials	√		

Comments:
Jody is very responsible about her own things. As her confidence grows, I will encourage her to take more initiative in the class.

Work and Study Skills

	Almost Always	Some of the time	Not yet
Follows directions	√	√	
Shows perseverance			
Takes pride in presentation of work	√		

Comments:
Jody takes pride in her work and is always very cooperative and eager to help others in the class.

General Comments:
Jody began the year as a very shy and quiet pupil. But as the year has progressed, I have been delighted to see the way she has grown in confidence. All her academic areas are progressing well-her reading is a real strength, and she loves the library!

Class teacher: *Ross Stanton*

Principal: *Milly Robinson*

Madison School Report

Name: Jody Yarnold

Room: 17

Teacher: Mrs. Robinson

Grade: 2 Year: 1998

Language

	Almost Always	Some of the time	Not yet
Listening and speaking			
Listens thoughtfully to the teacher and other children	√		
Listens to instructions and follows directions	√		
Speaks clearly so others can understand		√	
Speaks confidently in small group situations			√
Retells stories and rhymes		√	
Reading			
Enjoys a range of stories and genres	√		
Uses context clues to predict and confirm meaning	√		
Uses letter-sound clues to help predict and confirm meaning	√		
Understands use of capitals, period and speech punctuation		√	
Confident enough to take risk and make approximations		√	
Self-corrects own reading		√	
Writing			
Participates confidently in shared writing			√
Eager to write and express own ideas	√		
		√	
Has appropriate written vocabulary to express ideas		√	
Makes & checks spelling approximations, uses dictionary card	√		
Explores a range of genres and forms		√	
Forms letters correctly when writing	√		
Developing consistent handwriting style		√	

Comments:
Jody may be quiet but she reads eagerly and I have been very impressed with her stories (as you will see when you see her portfolio!). I have put her in a group preparing a puppet play at the moment and I have been very impressed with the way she is working with the group on that project. Everyone loved her poem about the beetle in the bathroom.

Mathematics

	Almost Always	Some of the time	Not yet
Enjoys math activities		√	
Works independently with apparatus		√	
Knows and understands basic facts and measures		√	
Applies mathematical understanding to solve problems			√

Comments:
Jody completed the measurement projects neatly and accurately. Her understanding of basic facts is growing. She really enjoys the activities with the math equipment and is developing good math vocabulary and ideas from that.

Science

	Almost Always	Some of the time	Not yet
Shows understanding of concepts studied		√	
Contributes effectively to group projects		√	
Asks questions that show an inquiring mind		√	
Seeks evidence to support ideas or conclusions			√

Comments:
Jody researched the frog project well. She is growing in confidence, but in group activities she still tends to let the others take the lead.

Social Sciences

	Almost Always	Some of the time	Not yet
Shows good general knowledge in class discussion		√	
Sensitive to others in the community	√		
Shows interest in other communities		√	
Contributes thoughtfully to class and group discussion			√
Applies research skills effectively to class projects		√	

Comments:
Jody's project on "People who Help Us" shows her thoughtful approach in this subject area. She listens well and as her confidence grows, so too will her contribution to discussion.

The Arts (Music, Art, Drama)

	Almost Always	Some of the time	Not yet
Listens to and appreciates a range of musical styles		√	
Contributes enthusiastically to class singing	√		
Able to sing in tune	√		
Expresses own ideas visually and with confidence		√	
Will choose from and employ a range of art media		√	
Skills: can cut and paste, paint, and draw with crayons		√	
Contributes with confidence to drama activities			√

Comments:
Jody has a lovely clear singing voice - she was chosen to lead our class singing last week. Interesting artwork, too. Explores use of color imaginatively.

Health and Physical Education

	Almost Always	Some of the time	Not yet
Participates and enjoys physical education activities			√
Runs, climbs, and does jump-rope with good coordination			√
Contributes thoughtfully to health topic discussions			√
Shows responsibility for own and others health and safety		√	

Comments:
Coordination is developing. Jody doesn't really enjoy the more boisterous activities.

Electronic Report Cards

Computers offer additional possibilities for reporting to parents. The Learning Assessment Record for each child is probably too large and unwieldy to give to parents on paper, but schools might want to offer parents updated disk copies of their child's Learning Assessment Record at particular points in the year, as a supplement to the traditional report card. Decisions about this will depend on how many students have computers in their homes. Of course, schools that provide individual laptops to their students will be well-equipped for this.

One approach is to send the disks home, along with a form inviting comments or questions, prior to meeting with the parents. The parents can then go over the record with the student and note comments and questions on the form. Then they meet with the teacher and discuss the student's learning, with the response form as a starting point and discussion framework. The teacher should have the student's records available as a hard copy or on screen at this time, along with the other assessment data the teacher has been collecting–the student's portfolio, teacher and student reflections, anecdotal records, etc.

The teacher might also want to consider making this meeting a three-way conference, by including the student (see the next section for suggestions).

An example of a Parents' Response Form is depicted on the next page.

Madison School
Wide Forest Valley

January 29

Dear Parent,

Please look at Jason's Learning Assessment Record on your computer and complete the form below.

Jason is really looking forward to showing you his own portfolio and all the other interesting things we have been doing this term.

Please return the form to school by February 5 so that I can finalize the conference schedule.

Yours truly,
Pat Watts

Parents' Response Form for the Learning Assessment Record

Survey Date: January 28
Student's Name: Jason Kliner

Dear Teacher,

I/we have looked through Jason's Learning Assessment Record on our computer. The following are three (or more) things that impressed us about Jason's work.

1.

2.

3.

I/we are concerned about:

I/we would like more information about:

The following are things I/we would like to talk to you about at our next parent/teacher conference:

Proposed conference date and time: Thursday, February 12, from 3 to 3:15 P.M.
YES ❑ I will be able to attend.
NO ❑ I will not be able to attend at that time. To help you find an alternative conference date, the following are good days and times for us:

____

Yours truly,

The Three-Way Conference

These updated versions of the traditional report card meet a number of the criteria we listed in our *Seven Habits of Highly Successful Teacher/Parent Communicators*–especially habits number 1, 2, 3, 4, and maybe even 5. But the report card doesn't really adequately deal with habits 6 and 7. They might encourage discussion between teachers and parents, but not necessarily collaboration or empowered participation (habit number 6). The information flow still tends to follow a one-way course, too–it's teachers reporting to parents, rather than the reciprocal flow of communication between teacher, student, and parent envisaged in habit number 7.

One way to encourage a much closer collaboration between teacher, student, and parent(s) is to report to parents using a three-way conference. The following is a typical procedure for such a conference.

The teacher completes a General Learning Progress Survey for the class. Then he or she sends a letter home to each student's parents, inviting them to participate with the student and teacher in a three-way conference and outlining the format for the conference (see the sample on the next page). Then the teacher and parents arrange a date and time for the meeting.

The teacher also prepares three forms: one for the student, one for the parent, and one for the teacher. These forms provide an opportunity for each participant to do some pre-conference reflecting and to jot down any thoughts, questions, worries, comments, etc. that each would like to share at the conference.

At the conference, the student introduces the parents to the teacher. (This is rehearsed in class prior to the conference so that all the students know how to make the introduction comfortably.) Then the student shows the parents the highlights of his or her portfolio and any other class projects displayed in the classroom.

The student, parents, and teacher then sit down together in the conference area of the room. The teacher facilitates the conference but gives as much responsibility to the student as possible. First they talk about the student's strengths. The student begins and says what has gone well so far in the current term. The parents are encouraged to share their perception of the student's strengths and comment on what their child has shared. Finally the teacher shares his or her perceptions of the student's strengths, offering data from the Learning Assessment Record and anecdotal notes where relevant.

Madison School
Wide Forest Valley

January 29

Dear Parent,

We'll be beginning our three-way conferences next month. This is where parent(s), teacher, and student all meet to talk about how school is going for your child and how we can all help. I'm really looking forward to it, and I know all the children have exciting things they want to show and tell their parents about, too.

I thought you might like to know what happens at these three-way conferences. First, your child will show you his or her portfolio and other things we have been doing this term. Then we will discuss your child's learning progress. We will be looking at three things.

- Achievements so far–the things your child feels good about.
- Challenges–the things your child might need help with or needs to improve.
- Goals–the things your child is going to try to work at next, and how we can all help.

There will also be an opportunity for you to comment and ask questions.

I have enclosed a form you can use in case you'd like to jot down some thoughts or questions before the meeting.

I look forward to meeting with you and your child next Thursday at three o'clock.

Yours truly,

Glenda Fox

The student is then invited to discuss areas that offer challenges or need more work or improvement. Then the parents comment, and finally, the teacher adds his or her remarks.

Then the student is encouraged to suggest, in the light of the discussion, several goals. The parents are asked to suggest ways in which they can help the student with these goals, and then the teacher offers suggestions on what he or she can do to help.

Parents' Preparation Sheet for a Three-Way Conference

Madison School
Wide Forest Valley

Parent(s)' Notes for the Three-Way Conference

Student:	Nadia Cole
Meeting Date:	Thursday, February 28
Time:	3:00 P.M.
Room:	14

Dear Parent(s),

Please use this form to jot down any thoughts or questions you might like to share and bring in with you to the meeting. Think about your child's:

Achievements so far–things your child should feel good about.

Challenges–things your child might need help with or needs to improve.

Goals–things your child might like to focus on and how we can help.

Any other thoughts, concerns, or questions?

Thank you,

Glenda Fox

Student's Preparation Sheet for a Three-Way Conference

Madison School
Wide Forest Valley

Student's Notes for the Three-Way Conference

Student:	Nadia Cole
Meeting Date:	Thursday, February 28
Time:	3:00 P.M.
Room:	14

Dear Nadia,

At our three-way conference with your parent(s), these are the things we are going to talk about. In order to prepare for the meeting, please jot down any ideas you would like to talk about under the headings. Bring this form to the meeting.

Your achievements so far–things you feel good about.

Your challenges–things you might need help with or need to improve.

Your goals–things you might like to focus on for next term.

Also, make sure you have your portfolio and any other special projects that you want to show your parent(s).

Looking forward to seeing you and your parent(s) at the conference.

Thank you,

Glenda Fox

Teacher's Preparation Sheet for a Three-Way Conference

Madison School
Wide Forest Valley

Teacher's Notes for the Three-Way Conference

Student: Nadia Cole
Meeting Date: Thursday, February 28
Time: 3:00 P.M.
Room: 14

Achievements:

Challenges:

Goals:

Decisions about how we can help:

The teacher brings the conference to a close by reviewing what has been decided and thanking the student for contributing to the discussion. After explaining that they'll all be working together to help the student, the teacher thanks the parents and tells them that, if there is anything they would like to discuss further in private, they should sign the sign-up sheet so that another appointment can be made. The teacher then tells the parents that a report on the conference will be sent to their home and they will be able to review how everything has gone next term or whenever the next series of three-way conferences is scheduled.

After the conference, the teacher spends a few minutes completing a Conference Report form. (See typical form on the next page.) He or she then uses this information to write a Conference Report. The student is encouraged to check the form and make any suggestions for additions or alterations. Then the student, the teacher, and the principal sign the report (with any amendments, etc.). The teacher makes a photocopy of the report (in case it becomes lost), and the student takes the original copy home for the parents to read and sign. This copy is brought back to school and photocopied again. The child then gets a copy, and so do the parents. The teacher keeps a copy of the report in the child's file and uses it for review purposes at the next three-way conference.

Teacher's Three-Way Conference Report

Madison School
Wide Forest Valley

Three-Way Conference Report

Student: ______________________________
Parent(s): ______________________________
Teacher: ______________________________
Date: ______________________________

Achievements discussed:

Challenges discussed:

Goals discussed:

How we can help:

Student:

Teacher:

Parent(s):

Signed

Student: ______________________________

Teacher: ______________________________

Parent(s): ______________________________

Principal: ______________________________

Chapter Review: The Teacher Personality Type Test

To find out what teacher personality type you are, answer Yes or No to the following questions.

YES	NO	
❑	❑	Does the sound of chalk scratching on a chalkboard make you think of violins?
❑	❑	Do you fantasize about your classroom when you are on vacation?
❑	❑	When you think of your students, do you break into a pirouette?
❑	❑	Do you begin to feel depressed and increasingly melancholy as the end of the school day draws near?

If you answered Yes to more than three of the above questions, then you are probably a *Romantic* type teacher.

YES	NO	
❑	❑	When you go out for a drive with friends, do you always remind everyone to buckle their seat belts?
❑	❑	Do you speak to store clerks, bank tellers, your spouse, and your father-in-law as if they were all the same age as the children you teach?
❑	❑	Do you straighten people's ties or smooth their collars when they're rumpled?
❑	❑	Do you find that when you talk about yourself to others, you use the classroom plural "we" instead of "I"? "*We think that's not a good idea. We think it would be better if...*"

If you answered Yes to more than three of the above questions, then you are probably a *Classical* type teacher.

YES	NO	
❑	❑	Do you always have to have every clock in the house set five minutes fast to ensure that you arrive on time–but you still always arrive 10 minutes late?
❑	❑	Do you sometimes secretly want to take your shoes off in the classroom, but don't?
❑	❑	Do you sing in the bath, in the shower, or while you drive?
❑	❑	Do you always have mountains of stuff on your desk? And do you keep saying, "One day I really have to clean this up!"–but you never do?

If you answered Yes to three or more of the above questions, then you are probably a *Creative* type teacher.

YES	NO	
❑	❑	Do you believe this test is scientifically sound?

If you answered Yes, then you probably: (a) know very little about science; (b) misunderstood the question; or (c) are dangerously gullible and need to read a good book on assessment.

Chapter 7

Getting Help

In This Chapter

- Murphy's Law: What Can Go Wrong Will Go Wrong
- When the Climate is Right
- Moving across the Philosophical Continuum
- Routines and Our Automatic Pilots
- Support Groups, Focus Groups, Local Networks, and Teams
- Some Handy Hints for a Teachers' Assessment Support Group
- Y. H. Prum's Law: What Can Go Right Will Go Right!
- Keeping the Community Informed and on Our Side
- Other Great Communication Ideas
- Frequently Asked Questions (FAQs) and Frequently Encountered Problems (FEPs)
- Help! I Don't Know If I'm Ready for This!
- Help! I Don't Know If My Students Are Ready for This!
- Help! The Other Teachers Want to Do It Differently!
- Help! The Parents Are Ganging Up on Me!
- Help! As an Administrator, Can I Manage This?
- Compiling Our Own "Help Desk"
- Chapter Review: Stress Markers for Traumatized Teachers

Murphy's Law: What Can Go Wrong Will Go Wrong

What we've been trying to do here is provide a systematic approach to a multi-strategied assessment process. One of the strengths of this system is that so much of it gets to be built by the people who have to use it. It's a case of: You knitted the sweater yourself for yourself, so it's most likely going to fit! But that doesn't mean there won't be the odd snagged stitch along the way. In this chapter, we're going to look at some of the most common, or most likely, snags and discuss ways to prevent them from happening, or at least correct or counter them so they don't unravel what we're trying to do.

We're working with people, and people have belief systems. Most of the difficulties we are likely to encounter with the introduction of this assessment process will come from subtle but often profound differences in beliefs about how teachers should teach and how students should learn.

Now, beliefs aren't always very rational. When in doubt, we humans tend to fall back on what feels right, and what feels right is usually what we've always done. That's why we tend to teach the way we've always taught (and even the way *we* were taught), and why the parents of our students so often prefer us to teach the way they "remember" being taught. I say "remember" in quotation marks because nostalgia is a wonderful editor and censor! So often we only remember the emotional high points–the good times and, of course, the bad times.

To introduce this assessment process will not only mean making changes in what we do but also in what we believe. To make those changes smoothly and effectively, we have to do more than just introduce a batch of appropriate procedures and practices–we also have to get the climate right.

When the Climate Is Right

These are some of the qualities we will need:

Security

Teachers, students, and parents need to feel secure. They need to know that the philosophy is sound, that the process has been carefully thought through, and that the results will justify the effort to bring about the changes. Everyone has to do their homework! They also need to be sure that this is not an "experiment"–that although there might be refinements and fine-tuning from time to time, this is the way things are going to be done for now and into the foreseeable future.

Collaboration

Working collaboratively means we have others to share ideas with, others to try our ideas out on, others to support us when we're having difficulties, and others to help us celebrate when things are going well. It just so happens that the others we need to collaborate with are all part of this learning enterprise: our students, our teaching colleagues, our school administrators, and our students' parents.

Ownership

Teachers, students, and parents all need to feel that they are participating and contributing–that this is not something being foisted upon them, but rather something they are creating and managing themselves. They have to feel valued and empowered and, in return, they must be committed and prepared to take significant responsibility.

Trust

There must be mutual trust between administrators and teachers, between teachers and students, and between parents and students and teachers. Each must respect the other's unique contribution. It's only when that trust is clearly there that people are able to be honest and fair with each other, and give and take genuine criticism and praise.

Communication

Communication is one of the most cliché-encumbered concepts in the world today. We all know the phrases: *My door is always open.* (That's because I'm always out!) *You can talk to me anytime.* (It just so happens I'm busy right now.) *Call me anytime.* (And leave a message on my voice mail.) *I'd love to hear your views.* (Put them on paper and leave them with my secretary.)

Seriously though, communication is essential in order for this assessment process to work. We need knowledge and understanding about communication; we need skills and strategies to make it happen; and we need attitudes and values that support and encourage it. We need to think about who we should be communicating with, and we should consider the most appropriate way to communicate. (Orally? In writing? Visually? Through body language?) We need to remember that communication is listening as well as talking. We need to be sensitive in so many ways–ethnically, culturally, politically, socially, in terms of age, gender, religion, and even favorite sports teams! And yes, in order to communicate, we also need a sense of humor.

Positive energy

There needs to be a sense of pleasure and excitement about what we are doing. Learning is one of the great human adventures. The more we enjoy learning and celebrate it and allow everyone to participate in it, the more enthused and excited everyone becomes.

Lifelong learning

There needs to be an attitude or state of mind that says we are all learners. Of course, the students are learning. But good teachers go right on learning every day, too. They talk about it, they model it, they let their students catch some of their own buzz and fervor. Parents are learning, too. They might be learning in their workplace or as a result of their own daily struggle to stay alive. But parents also learn about their children: "Who is this creature I brought into this world, and what does all this tell me about myself and *my* world?"

Moving across the Philosophical Continuum

As we mold and shape the philosophy that underpins our teaching, there are qualities we move away from, and qualities we move toward. The diagram on the next page shows some elements of the philosophical shift that is at the center of the assessment process and the philosophy of learning we have been describing here.

More of...	Less of...
More management	Less control
More facilitation	Less direction
More showing	Less telling
More modeling	Less instructing
More responsibility	Less checking
More collaboration	Less hierarchies
More goals	Less in the way of requirements
More ownership	Less bossing
More expectations	Less reliance on prescribed learning requirements
More ways to assess learning	Less testing
More assessment as a part of the learning	Less time spent on assessment tasks not related to learning
More diversity	Less stereotyping
More "The sky's the limit!"	Less need for bottom lines

Routines and Our Automatic Pilots

Of course, if we are intellectually challenging ourselves over every experience and situation we encounter in our lives, we'll soon start to suffer from a kind of cerebral burnout. That's why we have routines–habitual ways of doing things–so that we don't have to think about them every time we do them. Routines are also great because they give us time to think about other things. We have a kind of "automatic pilot," which we let take over the activities we are engaged in so that our minds and imaginations can roam freely at will.

As liberating as routines are, they are not without their traps. I personally solve most of the world's problems while I am shaving. While doing so, I usually get slower and slower, and of course, I am totally oblivious to family members lining up outside the bathroom door. What is even more unsettling, driving for me is another wonderful time for creative thinking. I have been known to arrive at the wrong destination simply because along the way I became so infatuated with some creative ideas that I let my automatic pilot take over and guide me down a routine–but wrong–highway!

We use automatic pilots in our teaching, too. We have routine ways of doing things and routine ways of thinking about the things we do. Problems can arise when we don't even recognize when we're on automatic pilot. In order to refine and deepen our teaching philosophy and be constantly upgrading and refining our teaching practice, we need to regularly reflect on what we do in our classrooms–and our reasons for doing it.

But it's very hard to do that on your own. The best way we can go about supporting and enhancing the effectiveness of both our teaching and our schools is to regularly share with our colleagues our professional knowledge and understanding, our skills and strategies, and our attitudes and values.

Support Groups, Focus Groups, Local Networks, and Teams

Setting up some kind of loosely knit group that meets regularly to reflect on teaching practices is one of the best ways to answer our questions and solve our problems. There are many names for this, and many ways we can go about doing it. Support groups, focus groups, local networks, and teams are just some of the names for such groups.

Ironically, it is often when we are trying to explain our problems and concerns to a group like this that we suddenly realize that we already know the answer ourselves. It's not surprising, really–in the hurly-burly of running our busy classrooms, we don't really have time to listen to ourselves. In a support group, we also have our ideas reflected back to us so we can hear how they sound and see how they look to other people. Sharing the exciting things happening in our classrooms helps keep us motivated, too.

In summary, we can gain much wisdom and practical knowledge from each other in this way. In fact, often the best consultants and the most useful professional development help is just across the hall!

The handy hints on the next page can make these support groups work effectively.

Some Handy Hints for a Teachers' Assessment Support Group

1. Set group meetings on a regular schedule so that they're predictable and have a Pavlovian effect on the intellect and the imagination.
2. Set rigid time frames. Always start on time and end on time. And don't allow the sessions to drag on. Few of us can talk about teaching philosophy and practice for too long without starting to repeat ourselves, and few of us can listen to someone else's soul-searching without becoming a little bored. Also, by shortening the time frame, you encourage people to focus and keep to the point.
3. Include something inspirational at each meeting. It might be a quote selected from a challenging professional book, an example or anecdote from one teacher's classroom, or a great idea for everyone to try.
4. Don't clutter the meeting with "housekeeping" matters. Do your nuts-and-bolts organization at another time or for a specified period of time only.
5. Keep the discussion tied to practical reality–what is going to work in your classroom with the resources that are available to you.
6. At the same time, have incredibly high expectations! In other words, be positive, and don't let the meetings get bogged down with problems or degenerate into "moan" sessions. Special tip: Outlaw the phrase, "Yes, but..." "Yes but..." means "No." If people mean "No," they should say so.
7. Think "sharing." This is a time when you share with your colleagues what you now know and understand, what you now can do, and what you now feel and believe about learning.
8. To help with hint number 7, hold these meetings on a rotating basis in each other's classrooms. Then you will be constantly reminded of what this is all about. It also means the teacher whose room is being used for the venue is able to easily share learning artifacts.
9. Think constantly: achievement, challenges, and goals. In fact, that is a good structure for these meetings. Set aside 10 minutes or so for sharing achievements (things that are going well), 10 minutes for challenges (things you need to improve or need help with), and 10 minutes for goals (things you're going to focus on next, and how everyone else can help).
10. Topic-based discussions should be held by mutual consent, but every now and then conduct a lottery in which everyone writes down what they'd like to talk about on a slip of paper, and one of those slips of paper is drawn from a hat.

Y. H. Prum's Law: What Can Go Right Will Go Right!

Readers who are "ambi-directional" will realize that Y. H. Prum is a close relative of Ms. Everything-that-can-go-wrong-will-go-wrong Murphy. Frankly, there needn't be any problems with the introduction of an assessment process like this. It could well be that all the exciting learner-centered things happening in our classrooms and in our school make this assessment process a natural development. In fact, in line with the principles we have reiterated here on a number of occasions–emphasizing the positive and having high expectations–maybe this chapter should have started with this section.

But we do want to sound one word of warning: Just because everything is going so well, it doesn't mean that we don't have to be wary. Human nature being what it is–or at least, the history of American education being what it has been–it's even possible for everything to be going too well!

To illustrate: We have methodically read through this book, thought about our assessment strategies, and completed our Learning Assessment Plans. We have begun to collect anecdotal information and helped our students to devise portfolios to document their learning. Meanwhile we've started teaching and planning and assessing and replanning–and everything is going superbly! The principal and the administrators are delighted. The students are excited. The parents think we're the greatest thing since whatever came after sliced bread! So, what could possibly go wrong?

It's all that hype and excitement. It can be almost as bad as too much doubt and negativity. Those who follow the stock market know that when things are booming and share prices are going through the roof, everyone starts to worry and say, "But when is it going to crash?" And, of course, it occasionally does, just as the doubters predicted!

Furthermore, like the stock market, American education is terribly prone to wild swings of opinion and is subject to rapid changes of fashion and confidence. What we are proposing here is an approach to assessment that we want to see sustained for the long haul. Obviously our approach will be refined and improved over time, but we don't want it to become politicized or polarized–something the public has to be either for or against.

Keeping the Community Informed and on Our Side

To prevent this process of assessment from becoming a political football, it is important to take our community with us through every step and stage. Everyone needs to be kept fully informed, and the place to start is with our students. They need to understand what we are doing and why. Not only does it vitally concern them, but also, one of the long-term goals of all assessment processes must be to enable students to internalize the processes and apply them in their own lives as part of their lifelong learning.

But there is also a more Machiavellian reason for this. We need to communicate effectively with parents, and for this purpose our students are often our best publicists, lobbyists, and advocates. If our students are excited about what they are doing at school and are eager to talk about school and share samples of work and other learning artifacts, their parents will be informed and start to feel that they are part of the learning process, too.

This "student publicity" is very valuable, but it is not enough on its own. We need to communicate directly with the parents, too, and make sure that this isn't just one-way communication. We need to enlist support, get responses, seek feedback, and invite participation.

We need to be sensitive and use the appropriate means of communication, too. It's pointless to rely on written reports if a significant proportion of our parents don't have strong reading skills, or if they aren't fluent in the language of instruction. If that's the case, oral communication might be more useful than written communication. Three-way conferences might be more appropriate than the traditional report card. A video log might be a valuable option for your community.

The school itself can be central to your "communication policy." Invite parents into the classroom. Have open house, or set aside one afternoon a week that is a public day. Have children take home the class log. Or if the class writes a Class Diary in shared writing, then let the children take this home in rotation and share it with their parents.

Above all, we should make the classroom reverberate with the learning! The walls should be rich with evidence of the learning experiences the children are having.

Other Great Communication Ideas

- If your school has an answering machine, at the end of each day enlist your students' help to record a message for the parents, giving an update on the day's news as well as the highlights of the week and information on upcoming events. Use rotation to make sure that each class gets a billing on this message.
- Make the school office or school entryway a focal point for the expression of the school's philosophy of learning–not in slogans or "teacher speak," but in examples of the philosophy in action. In other words, don't *tell* them what's happening and why, *show* them! Better still, let the students show them!
- Keep a photographic record of the highlights of the school year in the office so that when parents and visitors (including the students) are waiting, they can browse through it.
- Keep the media informed of upcoming events. Have a list of the people to contact at each local newspaper, and radio and television station. Keep a log of your calls and faxes to them and check the log regularly to make sure contact is being maintained.
- Create a school web page in which each class is represented, and involve the students in keeping it current.
- Encourage the students and other teachers to communicate with other classes and schools and share news and views. These could be schools in the neighborhood or in a completely different state or country.

Frequently Asked Questions (FAQs) and Frequently Encountered Problems (FEPs)

With all the best preparation and good will in the world, there are still going to be issues, questions, and even problems that will arise from time to time. In the remainder of this chapter, we will consider some suggestions for dealing with some of the more common of these. We'll group them in terms of where they seem to be largely coming from–from ourselves as teachers, from the students, from the other teachers, from the parents, or from administrators.

Help! I Don't Know If I'm Ready for This!

"I'm not a very experienced teacher. Can I really do this all by myself?"

Obviously it's easier to make significant changes in your teaching practice if others in the school are making similar changes–especially if you're a relatively inexperienced teacher. But the issue isn't really about whether we are competent to do this–it's more a question of confidence. With that in mind, check out your belief systems. If you agree with the principles and ideas outlined in this book–particularly the need for assessment to be a multi-strategied, organic (or integral) part of the planning and the learning–then the best way to prove you're able to do this is to follow the Nike slogan and "Just do it." The experience and confidence will flow from that.

Some suggestions, though:

- It helps if you can team up with another teacher–just so you have someone to share ideas with and thereby sustain your own enthusiasm and motivation. This doesn't have to be a teacher in your school. It could even be an "electronic buddy" with whom you correspond by e-mail.
- When deciding on your assessment strategies, make sure you include reflection strategies, not only for your students, but for yourself. And make sure you begin those reflection strategies with your achievements and the things you feel positive about.
- Follow the steps we've outlined in this book and reread the text whenever you're unsure or feel that you're loosing altitude.
- Keep a journal. When the going gets tough, look back in your journal to a time when things were going well. This will provide inspiration and motivation.

"I feel insecure about giving so much power to the students and to the parents. Will I be able to manage this, or will they gang up on me?"

Reread the section in this chapter on the climate necessary for these changes. Also, make a clear distinction in your own mind between power and control. The important power in your classroom is the power to *do something*, not the power *over someone.*

"It's taking too much time, and I need a life outside of the school."

If the process is being followed as suggested here, once the initial planning has been done, there should be less non-teaching time being taken up with assessment tasks, because so much of the assessment is done as part of the learning. But even the planning should take less time than many of the traditional assessment tasks, because you're planning the assessment while you're planning the learning, and the latter is something you have to do, anyway.

"I can't do this. I'm not computer literate."

It helps to have some basic computer skills. With a computer we can quickly calculate the totals we need for things like assessment summaries or subject or learner profiles. We can also design our own forms and response sheets. But all these tasks can be done just as easily with pen and paper and a copier. It might take a little longer, that's all.

On the other hand, if a computer is available for this task and you lack the necessary skills, maybe this is an excellent opportunity to gain some.

"I'm worried that, if I let the other teachers into my classroom, they'll steal my good ideas."

Collaboration means others will borrow our ideas, but it also means we're able to borrow theirs. It's a matter of attitude, and working in a professional climate. However, we can help ease our colleagues into collaboration by being scrupulously fair in acknowledging where the good ideas have come from. Sometimes this can be achieved informally in casual discussion by "naming" a particular idea after the person who came up with it. For example, *"I've been trying Joan's social studies response sheet and I find...."*

"What about the students with special learning needs? Will this assessment approach help them?"

The short answer is, "Yes, definitely." When teachers look closely at the learning and assess and document it methodically, they are able to be far more responsive to unique learning needs and divergent learning styles.

"My administrator wants to do the assessment for my class."

Maybe you could try to get your administrator to read this book! But if he or she won't oblige, the next best thing is to implement this assessment process as part of your class learning plan and let your administrator conduct the assessments he or she feels are necessary for administrative or accountability purposes. (It's not an ideal situation, but then you can comfort yourself with the knowledge that the other kinds of dinosaurs didn't last forever, either.)

"The administrators in my school pride themselves on being of the 'old school.' They don't trust these new-fangled approaches. Rather than using the Learning Assessment Record to do survey summaries, they say they're going to use the same old standardized tests they've always used. What can I do?"

This is really another version of the preceding question. The administrators are clearly not very secure or confident about all this, so unless you think you can get away with a palace revolution, the chances of changing their views by argumentation or philosophical opposition are slim. Try to get your administrators to read this book, but be subtle about it. Ramming it under their noses isn't likely to motivate them to read it sympathetically!

If all else fails, then let them do their tests. But use the range of strategies we've described here and develop your own Learning Assessment Plan and Record. Then you can use this to illustrate how simple and effective it is as a means of giving a snapshot of the class as well as providing the in-depth assessment information you need for effective learner-centered instruction. Perhaps when your administrators see the two side by side, they just might start to change their minds.

"An administrator wants to withdraw a child from my class because she or he thinks the child needs the help of a specialist, whereas I believe the child will be better off with the group."

This is where this multi-strategied assessment process is so helpful, because you will have so much evidence and documentation to show, reassure, and hopefully convince your administrator that what you are saying is sound.

Help! I Don't Know If My Students Are Ready for This!

"My students are used to being told what to do and how well they're doing it. They're not ready for this responsibility."

The only way to develop responsibility is to be given the opportunity to develop it. One of the greatest limitations to student achievement is not lack of student ability, but rather low expectations. Low expectations become self-fulfilling prophecies.

"I teach first grade–they're too little for this."

I have seen kindergarten teachers and their students doing all the things I write about in this book, and more. Don't kill learning with low expectations!

"My students are so excited, they want to put everything into their portfolios!"

It's wonderful that they're so excited, but the danger is that these portfolios can become just overwhelming collections of "stuff." The process of selecting and categorizing is one that has to be taught. One of the best ways to do this is to model it by having your own portfolio and "thinking aloud" as you decide whether you will or won't include something. Invite the students to help you with this decision-making. Get them to offer reasons for their suggestions. Also, praise student portfolios that show selection skills at work–this encourages the students to learn from each other. Encouraging your students to share their portfolios with students in other classes can be helpful, too.

Another suggestion: Don't have your students focus on choosing only their "best" piece of work. "Best" is a rather meaningless word. Try to get them to be specific. For example: *"I chose to include this piece of work because it shows how well I can now use people talking in my stories."* Or, *"I chose this piece because it's the first poem I've written this year."* Or, *"I chose this piece because I am proud of the diagrams I drew showing how the clouds work."*

One further suggestion: Set categories for what you want the students to include in their portfolios.

"My students keep wanting me to make their choices for them: 'Which piece should I put in my portfolio?' 'Is this good enough?' 'Have I finished this enough?'"

It's very flattering to be the font of all wisdom and arbiter of all taste in your own little classroom kingdom, but we do need to resist the temptation to be mother hen all the time. We need to nudge our students into making learning decisions for themselves. One of the best ways to deal with this situation is to reflect the question or request back to the student: *"Which piece do you think should go in your portfolio?" "What do you think–is it good enough?" "Do you think it is finished enough, or do you think there is more you can do with it?"*

It's important to do this in a positive way, though. The implication must be: *"I believe you are able to do this yourself,"* or, *"Great! Here's an opportunity for you to find out if you can really do this yourself! I'm sure you can!"*

"Some of my students come from very disadvantaged homes. Their parents never come to school conferences."

There are many reasons why parents do not come to school conferences, and often those reasons are quite complex. The parents might feel threatened or insecure about attending because of their own unhappy memories of school. They might feel that the school only wants to dump a new load of guilt on them for the problems their child is having. There might be complex family relationships that they don't want to discuss with outsiders. They might be shy. They might work in the evenings. They might be unable to speak English fluently. Whatever the reasons, we are the ones that must take the initiative and try to break down whatever barriers exist.

Some suggestions:

- Rather than beginning with a formal interview or conference situation, arrange a casual parent get-together such as a class barbecue for the first parent-teacher contact. If you suspect some of the parents are made nervous by the school setting, you might decide to hold this function at one of the parent's homes. It is very important to include the students, because they will make their parents feel at ease, and they can handle the introductions.
- You might also include any other children in the family, so that the lack of a baby-sitter doesn't keep people away.
- Come up with other non-threatening ways to help break the ice with parents who are uncomfortable around a school setting–make a special effort to invite them to things like school sporting events and concerts. Involving parents in making classroom learning equipment can be an excellent way to coax them into the school, too.
- Use your students for communication. Make sure they regularly take work home to share with their parents and seek parental involvement and response.
- Three-way conferences are very effective in making parents comfortable and helping them to feel that they're part of the process.

Help! The Other Teachers Want to Do It Differently!

"The teachers are adamant–they want to plan for just their grade, and they don't want to be part of a grade range planning exercise."

This is an attitudinal problem. Let them do grade by grade planning as the first step, and then combine those separate plans to make the grade range plan. This will be largely a matter of simplification, a question of seeing that the same learning outcomes are not repeated or duplicated within the range of grades.

"We're getting too many learning outcomes–it takes ages to just check them all!"

Yes, we did warn about this, didn't we. But "I told you so" doesn't help. It's counterproductive to have too many learning outcomes to check, because you end up spending all your time thinking about your assessment tasks rather than thinking about the students and their learning.

One way to avoid this problem is to set an arbitrary limit on how many preplanned learning outcomes you want for any given subject area. This compels people to make choices and prioritize. If someone is really wedded to a learning outcome and the other teachers are not, nothing is lost, because the teacher can still include that as part of the ongoing planning for his or her own class.

"The other teachers want to opt out."

This is a shame. Assessment is easier in a collaborative mode. But you can do it on your own, too. However, if the other teachers are adamant about dropping out, why not try to come up with a compromise situation: they can drop out, but they still meet with you from time to time so you can share your experiences with them and get the benefit of their professional knowledge and, hopefully, some support. (Of course, this is also a sneaky way to entice them back into the process later–next year, maybe!)

"The faculty members want to do this one step at a time, and the first step is portfolios–then we'll think about everything else."

As we have discussed in detail, portfolios are very useful things to have, but they aren't the whole assessment story. Too often, the move to portfolios comes about as a result of the search for a "test substitute." We've had plenty to say about that, too (see Page 24).

But maybe this statement should not be seen as a refusal to consider a broader assessment process, but rather as a message to school administrators that the teachers are under stress from too much imposed change. The teachers and administrators should be encouraged to read the sections in this book dealing with "ownership."

"Other teachers are cheating by inflating their 'consistentlys' in order to make their class and their teaching look good."

Of course, this gives a teacher only a short-term "halo." The next year's teacher is going to want to know how the teacher arrived at some of these inflated assessments! But rather than waiting for the wrath of next year's teacher, there are a number of things we can do in the meantime to help teachers be more consistent in their assessments of student learning.

- We can encourage teachers to regularly share, and thus compare, student work between classes. The main purpose of this is to share teaching and learning ideas, but teachers can also use this opportunity to talk about assessment criteria.
- Displays of work present another opportunity to make teacher assessment criteria more visible, especially if teachers are encouraged to write response comments on displayed work. For example: "*Thank you, Michael. One of the things I really liked about your story was the way you set the scene with your opening paragraph. You told me where we were, who was there, and what was happening. You had me caught up in the story right away.*"
- Exchange classes from time to time, maybe for specific projects or specific lessons.
- Exchange some students from time to time for specific projects or lessons.
- Experiment with "team teaching." For example, try pooling your two groups of students and teach them together for some subjects or topics.

"The teachers can't work together, or they don't want to work together, to plan the learning outcomes."

Factions and division in the faculty are difficult to deal with. Here are a few suggestions:

- Find the teachers who will work together and start planning with them.
- Split the task of defining the preplanned learning outcomes into sections, such as single subjects, and assign these sections to very small groups of teachers.
- Tackle the inability to work collaboratively first, and treat the assessment process as an opportunity to learn how. Choose a strong facilitator and proceed by setting highly precise and specific goals. For example: "*By the end of this week, we will have drafted 20 learning outcomes for kindergarten to third grade in science.*"

In one school with a deeply divided task, the facilitator decided to use humor and mock financial rewards. She invented a teacher currency called M&M dollars and rewarded and bribed the staff into working collaboratively. Each staff member was awarded a daily "salary" in M&Ms, but these salaries were paid to the students, not to the teachers. The daily salary was meager–not sufficient for a whole class. But the teachers could earn extra M&M bonuses by providing "random acts of kindness" to other faculty members.

Needless to say, since the students were the ones eating the M&Ms, they did their best to motivate their teachers to work together!

Help! The Parents Are Ganging Up on Me!

"The parents want grades and test scores."

It's important to deal with this issue early on, because if we don't, it only gets harder to explain later. It's also more helpful to be positive rather than negative, to concentrate on the values of this assessment process rather than spending a lot of time and energy saying what is bad about grades and test scores. The reason for this is that parents might be hankering after grades and test scores because those numbers and letters were part of their own personal experience. As a result, when you dismiss traditional assessment procedures with excessive vitriol, they might perceive this as a personal attack.

Besides, we need to do more than just explain or tell parents why we are assessing the learning in this way–we need to *show* them.

One way of doing this is to actually get them to do the assessment, too. For example, we can seek their observations and reflections on their child's learning; in other words, ask them to use two of the strategies we will be using in the classroom. To accomplish this, they will need to describe the learning with words rather than number grades, and document it with examples and significant instances, not test scores.

We also need to make sure the students understand and appreciate how we are assessing their learning, because they will then be able to explain it to their parents.

"Some parents don't believe their children aren't geniuses. They say there's something wrong with this new 'assessment stuff' we're doing!"

The problem here is that the parent has unreal expectations for the child. This occurred in traditional classrooms, too. But in the traditional setting, the problem was, if anything, worse because of the tendency to give children global labels like "gifted" and "talented." (Don't we all have some gifts and some talents, and so aren't we all gifted and talented?) Or "disabled." (Instead of a child who has abilities but who also happens to have a disability.) Or even "ADD" (see Page 2). The community tends to carry this labeling to extremes; hence the popular tendency to lump all human beings into one of two categories: winners or losers! Maybe all this came about because of the inadequacies of traditional assessment procedures. Maybe their very lack of specificity lead to such vague and imprecise categorization of people!

In our classrooms, the best way to deal with this situation is to avoid labels altogether and concentrate on describing the student's learning as accurately as possible and with examples and evidence to illustrate and back up these assessments.

"Some parents want their children to be classified 'ADD' or anything else to prove that it isn't their fault their children can't, or won't, learn."

The role of the teacher really becomes more of the counselor in these kinds of situations. We need to help these parents get beyond labels and see their children clearly and positively. Describing the learning specifically and being able to demonstrate learning progress over time will do much to reassure the parents. Help them concentrate on the positive. Start with what their children know and can do, and build on that.

"Some parents want the class to do less group work because the group is 'holding back' their children!"

We need to be able to demonstrate what our students are learning from group activities. Parents (and teachers) who are used to a very instructional approach to teaching might not be aware of how much valuable learning students gain from each other when the teacher is no longer at center stage and dominating the proceedings. A video log is an excellent way to convey this to parents.

Of course, we might need to do some soul-searching about the way we run our group activities. Are they really meeting learning needs effectively, or are we just impressed by how well we can run a three-ring circus? This is why reflection is such an important assessment strategy–it helps us challenge ourselves and grow as professionals.

"Some parents are threatened by diversity and independent learning. They don't believe that the children are capable of doing what the children want to do."

Parents who subscribe to a very strict, or even puritanical, upbringing might be uncomfortable with a classroom climate and teaching philosophy that encourages students to ask questions fearlessly and pursue independent lines of inquiry. We need to help parents see this questioning and independence as positive and necessary qualities for strong citizenship in a democratic society. We can best do this by showing rather than telling. We can model positive responses to independent learning in the things we say and the things we write on children's work. A video log is another valuable way to show how independent thinking fosters learning in the classroom.

"Some of my students' parents can't read."

We need to be wary of value judgments creeping into our attitude toward people who are unable to read. A nonreading parent can still provide enormously valuable experiences and support for a child. And it's important that the child sees that you value them for that, too. Regardless of whether or not the parents can read, encourage the children to read to their parents and share their school work with them. There might be other relatives or friends the child can read to, too. Another good idea is to arrange for your students to have "reading buddies" from an upper grade.

Note: When you're reporting to parents who cannot read, use oral reports. The video log is a good idea here, too (see Page 61).

"Some of the parents don't speak English."

Value the first language of the parent and the child. There are two important reasons for doing this: first, many important concepts will have been learned and thus will be imbedded in that first language; and second, by valuing their first language, you are also valuing the child and all those things that are part of the child, such as culture, ethnicity, and community.

Show that you value the language by taking an interest in it. Encourage the child to "be the teacher" and share phrases and expressions in his or her first language with you and the class. The aim is not to replace the first language, but to build English alongside it.

With regard to assessment, we need to be very sensitive and careful, because lack of confidence and facility in English can often mask or distort evidence of learning.

Help! As an Administrator, Can I Manage This?

"I have to run this school–that's my responsibility. But if we do this, will I lose control?"

It's important to make a clear distinction between control and management. To control, you need to direct others and limit both their power and their responsibility. With management, you empower others and share both the responsibility and the ownership.

"The other teachers are spending so much time on assessment-related tasks, they're neglecting their teaching."

If the assessment is being considered along with the learning and the planning, as we suggest, then the teachers shouldn't be neglecting their teaching. All the important aspects of teaching will be integrated and intertwined. In short, if assessment is keeping the teachers away from their teaching, they're doing it all wrong!

"The district has just spent a fortune on assessment materials or assessment consultants, and it doesn't want to abandon this investment."

The only investment that really counts is the investment in learning. In fact, in terms of cost, the assessment process we have described here is very economical. But you might not need to throw away all your recently purchased materials–maybe they'll give you some good ideas when you're planning your learning outcomes.

"As an administrator, I'm worried about what will happen when our students leave this school and go to another school where they are still using traditional assessment approaches. What records should we send along with the child? And will the child be disadvantaged?"

The best thing to pass on to the new school is the student's own Learning Assessment Record. This provides a snapshot of the child's learning to date that is very detailed yet easy to read and interpret. When it comes to planning appropriate instruction for the student, the new teacher will find the information on how the student matched up with the highly specific learning outcomes far more helpful than traditional grades with their abstract nature and often dubious reliability and validity. In fact, the child will be advantaged rather than disadvantaged.

"Call me old-fashioned, but tests have been around for a long time. How do we know some new-fangled approach is going to be any better?"

In fact, the standardized tests used in traditional assessment approaches are relatively recent creations. By contrast, the assessment strategies we talk about in this book have been around since our ancestors lived in caves. Cave dwellers would have assessed life-critical situations using *observation* and *interaction*. They also *re-created* their learning on the walls of their caves. To do this, they must have *reflected* on their experience. Maybe they kept "trophies" from their excursions into the real world, too, as *"learning artifacts"* to prove to other members of the community that they had mastered their survival skills well.

In other words, we're not really talking "new-fangled" here, but merely a systematic and common sense application of what we have known for thousands of years.

Compiling Our Own "Help Desk"

As we work through these challenges, we will also be learning and discovering our own solutions to the difficulties we encounter. It's a good idea to keep a log of these challenges and record how we deal with them–in part so that we can share them with other teachers who are embarking on the same assessment adventure, but also so that we can record our own professional growth and celebrate our own achievements.

One way to do this is to keep a Question Book. Divide each page into three sections. In the first column, we record the questions when they arise and note the date. In the next column, we record a number of possible solutions or ways of managing the issue. In the last column, we log how well these solutions worked out. The Question Book can be very versatile. It can be something an individual teacher keeps to log his or her own professional journey of discovery. It can be a collaborative document to which a number of teachers contribute. Or it can be used by all the teachers in the school.

Note: If a computer is readily available, instead of keeping this information in a book, we can store it on a computer file.

(See the sample Question Book entry on the next page.)

My Question Book

Question/Concern	Possible Solutions	How did it go?
9/4: I seem to be spending an enormous amount of time agonizing over the planning of my learning outcomes. (I'm doing this by myself. The other teachers don't want to do it yet. They want too see how I get along.)	9/11: Maybe at this stage, just to get things moving I should set some arbitrary limits–say 10 good learning outcomes for each subject area. That way I'll at least cover all subjects. And anyway, I can always add learning objectives later as it becomes clearer what the children need to learn.	9/25: I tried the 10 good learning outcomes idea. This worked fine. I've been working with the class for two weeks now, and already I can see a whole range of things. I should now add to my learning outcomes in my Learning Assessment Plan (LAP).

Chapter Review: Stress Markers for Traumatized Teachers

Research into teacher stress has revealed the following facts:

Fact Number 1: Teachers are very prone to stress.

Fact Number 2: Teachers are inclined to become even more stressed by Fact Number 1 because they are then driven to keep asking themselves the stress-inducing question: "Am I stressed?"

Fact Number 3: The most common treatment for stressed teachers is provided by other people telling the stressed teachers not to be so stressed–which, of course, makes them feel even more stressed.

Fact Number 4: It is a well-known fact that children are to stress what canaries are to gas in coal mines. Not only are they hypersensitive to teacher stress, but they are also biologically programmed to do things that only make it worse.

Fact Number 5: The last person to realize that he or she is stressed is the stresseee.

So, Are You a Stressed Teacher?

If you answer Yes to three of more of the following statements, you're probably suffering from mild to serious RSI (Repetitive Stress Injury). If you answer Yes to *fewer* than three of the following statements, you probably aren't involved in teaching!

- You spend a lot of time straightening things on your desk.
  Yes ❑ No ❑
- When sharpening pencils, you are inclined to sharpen away most of the pencil before you remember to take it out of the sharpener.
  Yes ❑ No ❑
- You find yourself repeatedly shouting at the class, "Stop shouting!"
  Yes ❑ No ❑
- Your class is suddenly quiet, and you just know it's a plot.
  Yes ❑ No ❑
- You can't find your desk. (It's buried under an avalanche of educational paraphernalia!) Yes ❑ No ❑
- You get to school and find that you're wearing socks that don't match, or you've put makeup on just half of your face.
  Yes ❑ No ❑
- You pack your bag or briefcase and drive to school, only to discover it's a holiday. Yes ❑ No ❑
- You set out to drive your own children to school, and discover when you get there that you've left them at home. Yes ❑ No ❑
- You can't remember the last time you laughed. Yes ❑ No ❑
- You're sarcastic with everyone, including your bank manager.
  Yes ❑ No ❑
- You find yourself even threatening to give God detention.
  Yes ❑ No ❑

Chapter 8

Getting Better and Better!

Assessment for Better Teaching: Assessment for Better (and Happier!) Teachers

In This Chapter

- Avoiding Teacher Burnout
- Teacher Self-Assessment
- Other Pick-Me-Ups for Tired Teachers
- Building Collaborative Strengths and a Learning Community
- Assessment and the Wider Community
- We're Doing So Well–So, Where Do We Go from Here?
- Chapter Review: Give Yourself a Giant Pat on the Back!

Avoiding Teacher Burnout

Throughout much of this book, our focus has been on how best to assess the learning and the learning needs of our students. We have made reference to the need for students to participate in their own learning, and that also means participating in the assessment of their learning. Students need to take increasing responsibility for their own learning. Rather than always relying on someone else's judgments about them (whether the judge is a parent, teacher, friend, partner, or boss), they need to be able to perform that validation for themselves.

But in this final chapter, we want to turn our attention to ourselves–the teachers and administrators who facilitate learning. Like our students, we are learning. Like our students, we need feedback to help us develop and grow professionally. Like our students, we respond particularly to positive feedback because it motivates us to carry on and try harder. Like our students, we need "artifacts" that remind us of our achievements and tell us we're doing OK. And like our students, rather than relying on other people's judgments about us professionally, we must empower ourselves with the confidence and strategies to be able to validate ourselves.

Why? Because teaching, which can be wonderfully rewarding, can also be one of the most demanding and exhausting careers. Teacher burnout can hit anyone–from the young, inexperienced teacher fighting day after day to manage a volatile and unruly group of youngsters, to the highly energized, super-achieving hotshot teacher who each day has to climb even more mountains than the day before.

The stresses of teaching come from many directions:

Unpredictability

We can plan and prepare meticulously, but there are always going to be those interruptions, catastrophes, and unexpected breakthroughs to throw our plans into disarray.

Constant change

Our students' understanding, skill level, morale, mood, and degree of motivation all change daily–sometimes hourly! We also have to deal with changes in the curriculum, changes in methodology, changes in teaching philosophy, changes in the people we work with, and changes in attitudes and values in the community we are responsible to. In fact, not only do we have to cope with constant change, but we are also actually expected to create it. If we are not changing the knowledge and understandings, skills and strategies, and attitudes and values of our students on a daily basis, then we aren't doing our job properly.

The repression of our own personal needs

No matter what is happening in our personal lives–be it a serious health problem, grief, financial worries, difficulties in our personal relationships, or emotional angst and despair–we still have a daily dramatic role to play in our classrooms of the positive, upbeat, we-can-cope, we-can-do-it persona. No wonder we sometimes hear our own inner voice from deep inside saying, "But what about me?"

The range of roles we play

We aren't just "the teacher." We're also the coach, motivator, model, personal trainer, and from time to time, the counselor, confidante, sage, mentor, military commander, police officer, judge, and jury. A Broadway star gets to play one role at a time. We have to play them all, often simultaneously.

Health risks

Our students kindly share everything with us, including their colds and viruses, their flu bugs and other infections, even their hair lice.

Teacher Self-Assessment

The bottom line is that teaching is a very stressful occupation. Frankly, unless we manage ourselves with great care, teaching can be hazardous to our mental and physical health!

In view of all this, it is important that we have strategies to cope with the stresses of our job. We can't just leave it to chance or finally seek help when the symptoms of teacher burnout become unbearable. We have to consciously plan to stay positively effective.

This is why our own self-assessment is just as important as the assessment we apply to the learning of our students. Just as we should be constantly and continuously assessing and evaluating their development, we should also be monitoring and regularly checking ourselves.

To do this kind of ongoing self-assessment, we need to use the same strategies we use with our students: observation, interaction, re-creation, reflection, simulation, and collecting learning artifacts.

Observation

To some extent we can "observe ourselves." We can step outside of ourselves and try to imagine what we must look like and sound like to an observer. Of course, self-observations of this kind are not always very reliable!

We can enlist the aid of our students. Having the students describe a lesson or a segment of work or the day will also provide indirect observations of the teacher. This is where a class log (see Page 57), and a video log (see Page 61) are helpful. Through these we will catch glimpses of ourselves as others see us.

Our colleagues who see us at work can give us observational feedback, too.

Interaction

Our interaction with our students is a useful source of information on how we are coping and how effective we are being. But there is one problem with this. In the words of Marshall McLuhan, "Fish don't know they live in water." Without someone to compare ourselves with, it's hard to evaluate how well we're doing. For this we need to see other teachers teaching, and especially other teachers working with our students. Yet too often teachers stay securely locked in their own classrooms. Their classroom kingdoms become classroom dungeons.

It's much healthier, and more professionally enriching, when teachers share what is happening in their classrooms in an informal and relaxed way. "Spontaneous sharing" should be encouraged. When something interesting is happening in your classroom, why not see if the teacher in the next room would like to bring his or her class in to watch.

Interacting with other teachers in team teaching, paired teaching, and variable space teaching can be helpful, too. All these methods provide excellent opportunities for us to learn from others. We learn about ourselves, too, because when we see other teachers dealing with familiar situations in similar and different ways, we start to appreciate and evaluate what it is that we habitually do in those situations.

We can also interact with ourselves. In other words, we can experiment in our classrooms. For example, we can try new management approaches or new teaching techniques and see whether or not they improve the effectiveness of our teaching.

Re-creation

Another way to check our teaching is to re-create it. A simple way to re-create a teaching experience is to tell someone else what you did. We can arrange to do this on a regular basis, using one of our colleagues as a "teaching buddy." We can also have an "electronic buddy," someone we correspond with via the Internet or e-mail. Support groups are helpful in this way, too (see Page 170).

Sometimes it's useful to express our response to teaching through other media–through art, for example. We can try drawing or painting ourselves teaching. It's not as silly as it sounds. Some teachers find this to be a very helpful way to discover and explore their feelings and thoughts about their teaching.

Another re-creational technique is to use your empty classroom to "replay" some incident from your recent teaching experience–perhaps something that has gone poorly or maybe even something that has gone really well. Walk your way through the experience again in order to re-create it, and talk yourself through it as you go: *"I was working by the blackboard here, and then the children said...."*

Reflection

Reflection is a vital assessment tool for teachers. We need to set time aside on a regular basis to reflect on our teaching practices. We need to think in a balanced way, too. It helps to think: *Achievements, Challenges, and Goals.*

We can also learn about ourselves from our students' reflections on their learning. Journals are a great help in this regard. Add flags to passages about the things that go very well, and on bad days, go back and reread those passages.

One useful reflective strategy is to wait until your students have left on Friday and then make yourself write about five things that you're proud of or that went well this week. Sometimes when we're feeling really blue we might be inclined to declare, "Absolutely nothing good happened this week!" When that happens, you have to be disciplined and tell yourself that you can't go home until you've thought of at least five positive things that happened during the week! Then on Monday morning, before you start the week, reread your list, just to reassure yourself and raise your morale. It can be helpful, too, if there is someone you can share this list with–a colleague, a friend, your family, or your partner or spouse.

Simulation

Tests are generally poor indicators of how well we're working as teachers. Standardized tests of student achievement might be interpreted in this way, but the validity of such an interpretation is doubtful, mainly because there are so many other factors besides our teaching effectiveness that can contribute to a surge or drop in student achievement. It is easier and far more valid and reliable to assess and evaluate what we actually do when we're teaching than to try to measure a simulated version of teaching performance using a test.

Collecting learning artifacts

Simulation isn't very helpful in determining how we're doing as teachers, but collecting learning artifacts certainly is. The artifacts we collect might not only provide documentation or evidence for the evaluations we make about ourselves as teachers, they might also give us an emotional lift. They can become like trophies, mementos, or even talismans, because in addition to documentation, they help evoke for us the excitement, pleasure, and sense of breakthrough that came with the learning.

There are many ways in which we can collect learning artifacts. We can keep our own "scrapbook" and include snippets of student writing and art, our own reflections, photographs, etc.

If we take a lot of photographs of our students, we can keep a photo album. If we have a scanner, we can scan the pictures into a computer and share them with the students. If we have a digital camera, we can keep an "electronic photo album" on our computer.

We can keep our own personal portfolio, including photos and exhibits that illustrate the contribution we have made to student learning through the year.

We can keep a journal.

We can make a display board in our classroom devoted to ourselves. We can explain to our students that everyone likes to feel special and encouraged in what they do–even teachers. The students might like to help by adding their own "commendations" for special things the teacher has done for them. Display photos of yourself or your family or your pets. Make a list of "Things I am Proud of this week." We might like to consider including some personal things, too: *"This is my family,"* or, *"This week was special because my son Jonah started school."* This activity is a good model for the Student Achievement Board, too.

Just as we might encourage our students to get their parents to display their work on a Home Display Board or the refrigerator, we can display our work at home. This will help keep family members and partners up-to-date with what is happening in our lives, and it can be a valuable starter for helpful conversations. Include inspirational quotes and stories, children's portraits of you, and things your students and the other teachers have said that have given you a lift.

Other Pick-Me-Ups for Tired Teachers

Goal setting

Goal setting can be an excellent way to keep a sense of momentum and purpose in our teaching. These goals should be achievable. (It's pointless to try to push ourselves to the equivalent of the two-minute mile!) They should be few in number. (Having too many goals becomes daunting and, therefore, counterproductive). They should have a time frame. (Set a date by which you intend to meet each goal.) And they should be written down. (This way, you won't forget them.)

Write your own report card

It's important to recognize and develop our own teaching strengths and improve our less successful areas. One way to help achieve this is to write our own report cards at the end of each term. List some key teaching areas, and for each area, describe your achievements and challenges, and set some goals.

Give yourself rewards

Sometimes it helps to give yourself special treats as rewards for your big achievements. (What qualifies as "big" will depend on you!) These rewards might be in the form of a special night out, a new hairdo, a new book, or some retail therapy–Saturday at the mall! But whatever the treat is, while you're enjoying it, keep reminding yourself why and how you "earned" it.

Have a school public-information strategy

It can be very validating and encouraging for teachers when the wider community hears about our good work. To achieve this, the school needs to be proactive in securing media coverage.

Parent meetings can also present opportunities for celebrating the teachers' achievements. What about a school newsletter or magazine as an opportunity to bring teachers' successes to the public's attention? Or a school page on the World Wide Web? Displays of student work in the school foyer can boost student morale. (But in addition to listing the students' names on these displays, include the teachers' names so that they get a lift, too.)

Too often all these things happen in a haphazard and unconnected way. But it's most beneficial when there is a definite school policy and plan of action to coordinate and facilitate positive publicity.

Parent Seal of Approval

Just as some businesses encourage their customers to applaud the work of individuals in the company, schools can solicit positive approval from parents. At the start of the school year, send each student's parents an envelope with about six "Seal of Approval" forms and a letter explaining what they are for. (See the following sample parent letter and sample "Seal of Approval" form.)

Sample parent letter

Madison School
Wide Forest Valley

Dear Parents,

We think Madison School is very lucky to have such wonderful teachers. Like everyone else, teachers like to know when others think they're doing a good job. To help in this regard, we have made our own Parent Seal of Approval. There are six Approval forms enclosed with this letter. During the year, if you think your child's teacher has done something really special for your child, or is doing a really good job in some way, please fill out one of these forms and send it to the school office. I will be very happy and proud to pass your praise on to the teacher.

Yours sincerely,

Jodie Mander
Principal

Sample parent "Seal of Approval" form

Madison School
Wide Forest Valley

Parent Seal of Approval

I would like to say a big "thank you" to my child's teacher,

Miss/Mrs./Ms./Mr. ______________________________

for doing that little bit extra by ____________________________

____

Yours sincerely,

____

Building Collaborative Strengths and a Learning Community

By sharing learning and assessment planning with our teaching and administrative colleagues, we also learn more about each other. We come to appreciate each other's strengths and recognize each other's weaknesses. With this knowledge, we can build on these collaborative strengths and collectively help minimize our weaknesses. By doing this, we also provide a valuable model to our students.

We can also involve the students and their parents in this collaborative partnership. We can share goals, draw on a wider pool of resources and experiences, and provide greater and more realistic connections between the learning we undertake in the classroom and the learning we need for life in the community outside.

Media commentators like to say we are in the midst of an Information Revolution. At times, it seems almost overwhelming. There is the immediacy of modern news reporting that takes you there–to the war zone for the military confrontation, to the operating theater for the medical breakthrough, to Mars to watch a planet yield up its secrets. Students still go to the library, but now they can use sophisticated computer search engines to help them in their research. Compact discs and computer data bases are stacked with information. Through the Internet, students have access to even greater layers of experience and information. Through electronic mail they can communicate with people around the globe, and with chat lines they can even communicate in real time.

Despite all these electronic advances, books continue to play a vital and exciting role in our children's lives. Publishers are producing more children's books than ever before. More writers and artists are working exclusively on children's books than ever before. There are more wonderful stories and poems and nonfiction books being created for children than ever before.

A consequence of all this informational innovation is that schools no longer have a monopoly on learning. As a result, the student's learning can be more integrated with the student's home life. Soon the traditional division between home and school might no longer apply. The learning from the school can continue at home. The experiences from home can contribute to the learning at school. And even when the school years end, learning will continue throughout the student's life.

In time, what we are in the midst of might come to be viewed not from the standpoint of the technology we are using (i.e., information technology), but what we are using it *for*. And for much of the time, we are using the technology to extend our experience and grasp of the world–in short, for learning. Just as the past had its Industrial Revolution and its Scientific Revolution, maybe this will in time come to be seen as the era of the *Learning Revolution*.

Learning has become a lifelong imperative. Business executives want to make their corporations "learning enterprises." The future growth and survival of a business depends on how quickly and effectively its leaders adapt and learn from their current experiences.

To cope with accelerating change, citizens need to be constantly learning, too. Learning no longer belongs to the witch doctors or the wise. In the modern tribal world, everyone must be a learner. If communities are going to grow and positively cope with change, they must be continually renewing themselves. They must become *learning communities*.

We must start this task by making our schools learning communities. Our students must know what it means to be a learner. They must do more than learn in a passive response to teaching. They must become active learners–learners who know how to learn, and how they personally learn best. Empowered with such an attitude, our students will cease to be passive absorbers of instruction and become partners in their own learning.

As part of this learning community, teachers become learners, too. They learn by observing and reflecting on their own teaching practice; they learn from their students; and they learn from their colleagues.

An essential component in all this learning is assessment. As learners, we need to discover our strengths, recognize our weaknesses, test our goals, document our achievements, record our learning progress, and define new and appropriate learning quests. All this requires assessment that is organic and is integrated with the learning. Assessment regulates the learning, but it also must nurture it, confirm it, and applaud it.

Assessment and the Wider Community

In Chapter 1 we looked at some serious misconceptions about assessment. Those ideas about assessment and the attitudes toward assessing and evaluating the learning are still strong out there in the community. One of the most important tasks we need to embark on is an effort to change some of those misconceptions.

We can start to do this through our students, by making sure they understand what we are doing and why, and what we are getting them to do and why. They in turn will be able to explain to their families the reasons and rationale behind this more organic learning assessment process.

We must work with our students' parents, too, and make sure they understand the principles that underlie what we are doing in the classroom. The best way we can do this is by actually involving the parents and having them participate in the process. Beyond that, we must be forthright with the media and make our schools transparent to the community.

There are some changes we as teachers need to make, too:

- We must constantly strive to keep our teaching "up-to-date," but at the same time resist falling victim to some poorly thought-out fad or fashion.
- We need to stop isolating ourselves in our classrooms and learn to work together more collaboratively with our colleagues across the hall.
- We must work with our administrators and give them grounds for trust so they will grant us greater ownership and responsibility.
- We should help the media to "assess" us in the same way that we are trying to assess our students–by highlighting and building on our strengths, and using measures of success that are based on documented authentic learning progress rather than statistically dubious test scores and grade levels.
- We must take our politicians on board, too. We must help them understand what we are doing and why, so that they can become our supporters and advocates.

We're Doing So Well – So, Where Do We Go From Here?

We've thought a lot about assessment and learning.

We've thought about how to integrate the planning, the teaching, the learning, and the assessment of the learning, and then the replanning, etc.

We've thought about who we are doing this for and why.

We've planned the learning.

We've planned the assessment strategies and chosen the learning tools we need to assess the learning.

We've observed and interacted and re-created and reflected and simulated and collected learning artifacts.

We've recorded our assessments anecdotally and over time, and we've kept a Learning Assessment Record.

At regular intervals we've completed snapshot surveys to help our administrators keep a clear grasp of accountability issues.

We've encouraged our students and their parents to be partners in the assessment and learning process.

We've reached out to the wider community and sought to change attitudes toward learning and assessment in the interests of developing a learning community.

We've considered our own professional health and well-being.

What should we do now?

We should feel very proud of ourselves. We're doing a good job. Isn't it about time we gave ourselves a giant pat on the back?

Chapter Review: Give Yourself a Giant Pat on the Back!

Now, this is an activity we can do with our students. But just for fun, maybe we can do it for ourselves, too.

Draw a giant hand on a piece of cardboard and then cut it out.

Examine your own hand. There are at least 14 segments that make up your fingers and thumb.

You ought to be able to think of at least 14 things you can feel proud of in your teaching.

As you think of them, write them down on your "giant hand."

Look at your own hand again. Across the palm and inner section of your hand are some long lines. Fortune-tellers look at those lines for clues as to what has happened to us in the past and to predict exciting things for the future.

Do the same with your "giant hand." Draw some lines and note the high points in your teaching career so far. That's your past.

But now be bold and add some predictions for the future.

What do you do now? Why, you take your "giant hand" and pin it to your own personal bulletin board or attach it to the refrigerator with magnets.

Well done! You deserved that Giant Pat on the Back!

Bibliography

Clay, M.M. 1985. *The Early Detection of Reading Difficulties* (3rd Edition).
Portsmouth, New Hampshire: Heinemann.

Clay, M.M. 1991. *Becoming Literate: The Construction of Inner Control.*
Portsmouth, New Hampshire: Heinemann.

Clay, M.M. 1993. *An Observational Survey of Early Literacy Achievement.*
Portsmouth, New Hampshire: Heinemann.

Davies, A., Cameron, C., Politano, C., and Gregory, L. 1994. *Together is Better: Collaborative Assessment, Evaluation and Reporting.* Armadale, Australia: Eleanor Curtain Publishing.

De Fina, A. 1992. *Portfolio Assessment: Getting Started.*
New York, New York: Scholastic Professional Books.

Goodman, K., Goodman, Y., and Hood, W. (Editors) 1989. *The Whole Language Evaluation Book.*
Portsmouth, New Hampshire: Heniemann.

Goodman, K., Shannon, P., Freeman, Y., and Murphy, S. 1987. *Report Card on Basal Readers.*
Katonah, New York: Richard C. Owen Publishers.

Green, A., Lane, B. (Editors) 1994. *The Portfolio Source Book.*
Shoreham, Vermont: Vermont Portfolio Institute.

Harp, B. (Editor) 1994. *Assessment and Evaluation for Student-Centered Learning.*
Norwood, Massachusetts: Christopher-Gordon Publishers.

Hein, G., Price, S. 1994. *Active Assessment for Active Science: A Guide for Elementary School Teachers.* Portsmouth, New Hampshire: Heinemann.

Hill, B., Ruptic, C., 1994. *Practical Aspects of Authentic Assessment: Putting the Pieces Together.*
Norwood, Massachusetts: Christopher-Gordon Publishers.

International Reading Association, Inc., 1995. *Reading Assessment in Practice. Book of Readings.*
Newark, Delaware: International Reading Association, Inc.

Johnston, P. 1997. *Knowing Literacy: Constructive Literacy Assessment.*
York, Maine: Stenhouse Publishers.

Learning Media Limited, 1997. *Reading for Life–the Learner as a Reader.*
Wellington, New Zealand: Learning Media.

Ministry of Education, 1985. *Reading in Junior Classes.*
Wellington, New Zealand: Learning Media.

Pigdon, K., Woolley, M. (Editors) 1993. *The Big Picture: Integrating Children's Learning.*
Portsmouth, New Hampshire: Heinemann.

Porter, C., Cleland, J., 1995. *The Portfolio as a Learning Strategy.*
Portsmouth, New Hampshire: Heinemann.

Traill, L. 1993. *Highlight My Strengths: Assessment and Evaluation of Literacy Learning.*
Crystal Lake, Illinois: Rigby.

Trussell-Cullen, A. 1997. *Inside New Zealand Classrooms.*
Katonah, New York: Richard C. Owen Publishers.

Valencia, S., Hiebert, E., and Afflerbach, P. (Editors) 1994. *Authentic Reading Assessment: Practices and Possibilities.* Newark, Delaware: International Reading Association.

Vopat, J. 1994. *The Parent Project: A Workshop Approach to Parent Involvement.*
York, Maine: Stenhouse Publishers.

Index

A

B

C

L

M

N

O

P

Q

R

S

T

V

W

Y